IF YOU CAN'T

LOSE IT,

DECORATE IT.

IF YOU CAN'T
LOSE IT,
DECORATE IT.

And other hip alternatives to dealing with reality

Anita Renfroe

NAVPRESS®

BRINGING TRUTH TO LIFE

OUR GUARANTEE TO YOU

We believe so strongly in the message of our books that we are making this quality guarantee to you. If for any reason you are disappointed with the content of this book, return the title page to us with your name and address and we will refund to you the list price of the book. To help us serve you better, please briefly describe why you were disappointed. Mail your refund request to: NavPress, P.O. Box 35002, Colorado Springs, CO 80935.

The Navigators is an international Christian organization. Our mission is to advance the gospel of Jesus and His kingdom into the nations through spiritual generations of laborers living and discipling among the lost. We see a vital movement of the gospel, fueled by prevailing prayer, flowing freely through relational networks and out into the nations where workers for the kingdom are next door to everywhere.

NavPress is the publishing ministry of The Navigators. The mission of NavPress is to reach, disciple, and equip people to know Christ and make Him known by publishing life-related materials that are biblically rooted and culturally relevant. Our vision is to stimulate spiritual transformation through every product we publish.

ISBN-13: 978-1-57683-994-2
ISBN-10: 1-57683-994-X

Cover Design: Brand Navigation, DeAnna Pierce & Bill Chiaravalle
Cover Photo: Don Jones Photography www.donjonesphotography.com
Creative Team: Terry Behimer, Traci Mullins, Darla Hightower, Arvid Wallen, Pat Reinheimer

Some of the anecdotal illustrations in this book are true to life and are included with the permission of the persons involved. All other illustrations are composites of real situations, and any resemblance to people living or dead is coincidental.

Unless otherwise identified, all Scripture quotations in this publication are taken from the HOLY BIBLE: NEW INTERNATIONAL VERSION® (NIV®). Copyright © 1973, 1978, 1984 by International Bible Society. Used by permission of Zondervan Publishing House. All rights reserved. Printed in the United States of America. Other versions used include: *THE MESSAGE* (MSG). Copyright © 1993, 1994, 1995, 1996, 2000, 2001, 2002, 2005. Used by permission of NavPress Publishing Group.

Published in association with the literary agency of Alive Communications, Inc., 7680 Goddard Street, Suite 200, Colorado Springs, CO 80920 (www.alivecommunications.com).

Renfroe, Anita, 1962-
   If you can't lose it, decorate it and other hip alternatives to dealing with reality / by Anita Renfroe.
      p. cm.
   ISBN 1-57683-994-X
   1. Christian women--Religious life. I. Title.
BV4527.R45 2007
248.8'43--dc22
                              2006038048

Printed in the United States of America

3 4 5 6 7 8 / 11 10 09 08 07

FOR A FREE CATALOG OF NAVPRESS BOOKS & BIBLE STUDIES,
CALL 1-800-366-7788 (USA) OR 1-800-839-4769 (CANADA)

table of contents
tablecloth of contents
crocheted doilies on top of
the tablecloth of contents
complete with fabulous place
settings and ornate centerpieces

if you can't change the picture, try a new frame

Don't you just love the movies? Good ones, I mean? I do. There's something about the process of deciding which flick looks promising, hopping in the car with a friend, purchasing your tickets, getting them torn in half by an embryo (by that I mean a high school sophomore who has no idea how anyone *your age* even has a social life at all). You are then faced with a serious statistical improbability, that being your ability to pass up the popcorn at the concession stand. I'm not sure if there is some sort of olfactory equivalent to cocaine, but the smell of popcorn at a movie theater would qualify in my unscientific book. It's irresistible and addictive. Of course, these days it takes a small second mortgage to *afford* the concessions. (In addition to your garden variety buttery popcorn and a soda, you can now partake of gourmet pretzels, nachos, bottled water, and cappuccinos—this is what is wrong with America: too many choices. But I digress.)

We find our way to Theater 23, shuffle our way up the dark ramp, and allow our eyes to adjust to the darkened room. We gingerly climb the stairs to the seat we hope will make this viewing experience perfect. Not too far away (too many heads to look past) nor too close (neck ache!). We are then subjected to 14 minutes of trailers for upcoming movies ("trailer" is French for "we used all the great dialogue in the advertisement so don't bother paying for the full version—you've already seen all the good parts"). In my experience it seems that this 14-minute-trailer segment is the exact length of time it takes me to get down to the unpopped kernels portion of my bag. Bummer! *Prematura popcorna eatemupus* bests me again. For the people who may have just come to this country from another country without movie theaters, we have to sit through the premovie announcement regarding the location of emergency exits, the availability of theater gift certificates, and how cell phones should be turned off or put on silent—especially those very precious persons who think the world cannot function without their presence for NINETY STINKIN' MINUTES . . . um . . . wow. Let me put my soapbox back under the chair. There. Now, where were we? Oh, yes, this premovie announcement is where I find myself in a perplexing dilemma regarding the disappearance of my popcorn. Should I get up, go to the concession stand, and get my free refill and risk missing the first 2.5 minutes of the movie—the plot and character establishment—the most important part (other than the last 2.5 minutes of a movie, when I am wondering if I will be able to hop with my legs crossed down the stairs, down the ramp to the ladies room as my Coke would like to exit *now*) or just sit here and have no popcorn for the actual movie itself? I can tell you now that my curiosity will usually trump my appetite and, boy, am I ever ticked if it's one of those movies that starts with lots of scenery and credits.

Finally, I am settled in to a place where I am temporarily transported to another world. Ah, movies. I especially love the ones that put the "move" in "move-ies" — the ones that really "move" me. They cause us to feel things, empathize with characters. Sometimes we identify so strongly with certain characters that we freely quote from them, occasionally doing full-on vocal impersonations (witness any male attempting Brando in *The Godfather*: "You go to the mattresses," or Stallone in *Rocky*: "Yo, Adrienne"). I quote from movies all the time to solidify my points with people. It's almost like emotional shorthand, unless you are talking to someone who isn't a dialogue junkie, in which case you have to stop and explain the context (or the whole movie, for that matter), in which case it's not worth the verbal energy. You know what I mean.

I especially dig movies that deal with the subject of "what is real." We have *The Wizard of Oz*, where Dorothy could testify on a stack of Bibles that the cast of characters she met in Oz were "as real as me and you"; *The Matrix*, where what seems real is more of a computer-generated coma to opiate the masses; and *A Beautiful Mind*, that depicts what happens when the wall that separates actual people and events from those that an overactive imagination can create begins to crumble. In each of these movies the main character had to make a choice about coming to grips with reality.

By the time the credits roll and the lights come up, we do, too, as we know it's time to throw away the popcorn bag and 32-ounce cup and return to our life. Such as it is.

So when the lights come up and the post-theater journey begins, what is your reality? I would be willing to bet that you're not famous, glamorous, inordinately wealthy, pampered, or physically perfect. I would also be willing to bet that you have occasional bouts of serious doubts about the importance of your life and whether or not you have done anything with it that really matters. You may feel that you aren't really living the life you had envisioned (who is?!) and that you wake up every morning in someone else's dream because you have made decisions based on someone else's priorities or feelings and now you are living with the consequences. You've fallen down the proverbial rabbit hole. And it's all too real.

But I do have good news.

My grandmother had all sorts of wisdom that she would dispense in her own, countryfied way. Whenever she was trying to help me understand that my perspective on a recent scrap with one of my cousins might need a little adjustment, she would say to me, "Anita, you know there are actually three sides to every story: there's your side, there's the other person's side, and then there's the truth. Most likely it's somewhere between your side and your cousin's side, but only God knows what it really is."

For most of us, we can breathe a sigh of relief, knowing that only God knows the truth of our lives. He's seen the whole shootin' match and, interestingly enough, He sees all that's coming up, too. And you know what? He's so incredibly in love with us. He knows how many cellulite stripes we possess on which body parts, the candy we stole from our best friend's desk in third grade, our incredibly stubborn streak, the number of hairs on our head, AND their original color. He knows it all. And He is not rejecting us nor abandoning us. The fact that we're still breathing is proof that He is not finished with us and that we have something purpose-filled to do on this earth with the days we have left.

So what's a girl to do with the reality of her life? Should she deny it and pretend that her life is better than it really is? Should she cry (or worse) about it because she can't change the way things are? Should she determine to just accept it—in a resignation sort of way? I say, "Nay, verily, nay!" (It sounds more biblical that way.) We must resist the urge to stop at *mere acceptance* of our lives. It is completely lacking in imagination. No. We must, instead, reach deep down and get in touch with every woman's Inner Crafter and begin to *reframe our reality*! Bling it up, so to speak. We need not waste another moment believing that we are just plain ordinary and that all of the "really important" work is being accomplished by someone more gifted, more respected, more wealthy, more visible! You and I are living an incredible life right now—we may just need to give it a little decoration in order to appreciate its dazzle.

That's why I'm here—to take you on a walk-through of your life, to see which parts of it you may not have fully accepted and certainly never considered worth decorating.

Before we get started, I must put forth a couple of minor disclaimers.

Disclaimer #1: I am not a decorator.

This is a widely known, objective, empirical fact. My only decorating knowledge can be summarized in three easy principles:

1. Do not mix plaids with polka dots. It will not be considered "eclectic and cool" unless you are Mary Engelbreit. Not only can she get away with it, she makes a kajillion dollars a day selling stuff with polka dots and stripes all over it. If you are not her, don't try it. It will only serve to prove you are a Decorating Dork.
2. You can't apply water-based paint over the top of a prior coat of oil-based paint. (I've tried. It beads. Badly. Then you are stuck with unintentional polka dots. Not good.)
3. Decorating elements make a stronger statement when grouped together.

I know numbers 1 and 2 through trial and error. I heard number 3 on *TLC, HGTV,* and from salespersons trying to sell me groups of things.

I've had plenty of chances to express myself in the area of Amateur Interior Design as our first homes were, well, very first-y. When John and I were newlyweds we lived in a duplex at our college. It was three rooms, but we managed to piece together enough furniture to make it comfortable, and I have vivid memories of stenciling little hearts in the bathroom. Does it get more Obviously Newlywed than hearts stenciled in the bathroom? It was as if our love was so strong that it spilled forth upon the walls like the Sistine Chapel, only a little less refined. We didn't really have much to go on the walls, but, then again, there wasn't much wall space to fill. I was into rainbows and panda bears as my theme in the kitchen. I cannot explain this other than I was still under a latent influence of the music of Big Bird.

When we moved from our duplex onto the church field, we were given a little "pastorium." For those of you not familiar with the term, "pastorium" is Latin for "It's free rent, get over it already." It was significantly larger than the duplex, but it had carpet and linoleum from 1969 (which would have been fine if it wasn't 1984). So we tried to decorate around harvest gold and avocado green as best we could. This phase of my decorating life could be best described as Sheets Make Fine Decorating Sense period. Not only could you sew a single seam onto a pillowcase and have coordinating throw pillows, but I somehow figured out that the top edge of the sheet could fit onto a curtain rod, and I had sheet curtains everywhere. I also graduated from stenciling hearts to stenciling geese. Country geese formed the borders of many walls. They were everywhere, these stenciled geese. On the breadbox, on the hand towels, on the salt shakers, paper towels, toilet seat lids. I will not even begin to analyze what that might mean psychologically.

Our next move was to the first house we built and owned, so we got to choose the paint and floor coverings for that one. It seems exhilarating and empowering, but by the time you get to the finishing stage of any house (and this is The Immutable Law of Home Construction), you are out of money. Any fabulous notions that you had in the beginning now seem financially irresponsible.

So you are weighing your options: "better carpet pads and chair rails or $75 less on the monthly mortgage for twenty years?" We opted for "builder's grade" (read: "super cheap") everything. We still didn't have much furniture to speak of, but fortunately/unfortunately for us, this was a decade when wallpaper was considered tres chic so we embarked upon our Wallpaper Is The Decorating Solution phase. We papered it all. I do not recommend this as a project to take on with your spouse if you are spatially impaired, diametric opposites in personalities, or if either one of you is irresponsible with an X-acto knife. I was under the impression that the blue line we snapped for a plumbline was just a suggestion. Creative people can't understand why little things like inches matter. So we learned fairly quickly to start in the most obvious corner of the room and finish up in the least obvious corner of the room because, by the time you get to the last corner, you will be eeking out the last of the roll of wallpaper so you don't *have* to buy another roll or you will find that your walls aren't square. I always went with the "not square walls" defense rather than admitting that the plumbline was accurate after all. We survived this wallpaper phase and suspect that the wallpaper glue may have been laced with hallucinogenics. This would be the only explanation for our pattern choices.

We moved again and for the next five years I would say that my life was dominated by the Hunter Green and Burgundy Phase. It was the first time we bought matching pieces of furniture and these deep colors were on them all. Every room, same two colors. Maybe I was trying to atone for the Geese Years. Maybe it's because all three of my children had been born by this time and these colors do not show dirt. I also discovered "crate" furniture. It was made out of heavy pine, it was virtually indestructible, and it came with hunter green cushions. Add burgundy colored throw pillows and, voila! Decorating done. Well, not exactly.

As with all home fashion periods, as soon as you have acquired The Total Look (meaning that you are thematically unified, and you can no longer find further accessorization), the clock starts ticking, sorta like a little internal hourglass, and you've got approximately twelve to eighteen good months before you are one day struck by the thought that you are completely tired of it. I mean DONE. But you can't afford to start from scratch, so you transition from one look to the next by sneaking in pieces of the next period while you phase out the last one. Thus was my transition to the Laura Ashley Floral on Everything Years. It started off innocently enough with a floral throw pillow or two and ended up with us living in Maniacal Botanical Land. These years were particularly hard on my husband and boys as they felt less-than-comfortable eating off floral plates that were sitting on a floral tablecloth in a floral-papered dining area. There was floral potpourri atop every toilet and floral prints hanging over the floral and striped couch. I distinctly recall wearing Victorian doily socks and floral jumpers that caused me to fade into that couch whenever I sat upon it. Perhaps I was subconsciously trying to hide from the children.

I am now in my This is My Last (Whatever) Phase. I say "whatever" because as we are shopping for furniture now I am looking for nice neutrals or very sturdy, long-lasting pieces that I don't have to replace inside the next twenty years. Or as John likes to bottom-line it, "Can you imagine yourself dying on this (bed, couch, recliner, table, chair, rug, lamp)?" It seems sort of morbid, but I think we're both just not interested in doing another decorating phase for the rest of our lives. Maybe that's one definition of "old," and I am beginning to understand the logic behind all the plastic couch covers in retirees' homes.

All that to say, I've had plenty of opportunity to develop my decorating life, just not much success at it. In fact it is common knowledge that my husband is much better at the whole decorating thing than I am. He routinely "rotates" our decorations, meaning that he will take some decorating elements and put them in the attic to make room for other things (like we're the Smithsonian and we can't possibly display everything we have). This is partly due to his tendency to squirrel things away (he's "saving" them), and he will occasionally go up there, bring something down, and exclaim, "Look what I found while I was up in the attic." He is certain that I will be excited at his "find" (he didn't "find" it since he's the one who put it up there), but 89 percent of the time it is something he has "rotated" to the attic and forgotten to take out the next time that season rolled around, and in the four years that have passed since he placed it up there, my tastes have evolved to the point that I don't even *like* said item anymore. The thing that really gets my blood pressure up is that during the period *when I used to love it and I would have enjoyed it*, IT WAS IN THE ATTIC. Languishing there in the heat and the cold for several years until I am totally over it. I have a fear that one day the "rotated" items are going to add up to too much weight and we will all be crushed beneath the resentful, vanquished pieces. If you hear that we met our demise in this fashion, remember to tell the Suspicious Death Investigators what really happened.

Disclaimer #2: I am not a total Pollyanna.

I will readily admit that I lean a little hard to the Sunny Side of Life. And I know that can be annoying to the people who lean the other way (see chapter 6). I prefer to think that I am more likely a "reluctant optimist." I am aware it's more chic to be upset and crusading and looking for all the things that are wrong so that we can try to fix them. There are plenty of people who write books about that stuff. I read them and I believe that there is much wrong with the world. But I also believe that more may be *right* with life than we have been conditioned to see. I'm not sure if the glass is half full or half empty (I've found that if I stare at said glass long enough, it's usually both). I'm just saying that you can choose a better-looking glass for the half full/half empty contents. I know you stand in front of your cabinet and do the same thing I do—look for your favorite glass or mug to drink out of. Why do we do that? Like the container changes the contents? Not one iota—just that the experience of drinking from it is greatly enhanced by the container. This seems fluffy and unspiritual, to choose to reframe our life so that we enjoy the contents more because of how we contain them, but we are called to a life of faith that sees things beyond reality. My life is what it is, and so is yours. I have had hurts, so have you. Will "decorating" your reality change it from a two-bedroom ranch to a six-bedroom mansion? Not a chance. I know that when we were given our first living quarters (as they were rentals), we were totally incapable of changing the structure of those houses. We could not make any noticeable changes from the outside looking in, but we had every freedom to make the inside what we wanted it to be. To stencil geese, to put sheets in the windows, in short, to make it home. It didn't change the view looking in, but it changed everything about the view looking out.

So, Gentle Reader, we are now ready to commence our Life Decor discussion. I call it that because I will be throwing out my opinions and you will answer me in your head (don't do it out loud or you will get very strange stares). I am happy that you have chosen to read the words that I am pounding out on my itty bitty laptop. So let me dust the crumbs from my Pepperidge Farms Milano cookies off the screen so I can see where we're headed. Ah, yes—the territory that lies somewhere between the heart and the funny bone. Let's go!

if all the world's a stage, can i get Oprah's lighting?

I t was all over the news for a couple of weeks—the story about how the fashion moguls in Spain refused to allow abnormally thin models to run their catwalks. The Spanish Association of Fashion Designers' protest over the industry's preference for waif-thin and "heroin chic" models whose hip bones, collar bones, and rib cages stick out like concentration camp victims was met with outrage by some. I heard several interviews with representatives from various high-profile modeling agencies saying that this was a form of discrimination against the "naturally thin" models. One of the interviewers asked the question, "Instead of rapping them on the knuckles and telling them to go home, why don't we find a way to celebrate women of all sizes?"

Why not, indeed.

I think it would be enormously refreshing to see women on the runways of New York, Milan, AND Madrid who were every size number from 2 to 22, just to drive the designers a little batty. A friend of mine who watches the TV show "Project Runway" said that in one episode the wannabe designers were "forced" to design clothing for "real women," who happened to be the moms and sisters of the designers. Some of them were on the verge of emotional breakdown as they had to create something to accommodate curves instead of hang from a pole. I only wish she had called so I could have TiVo'd it.

They say that the average size woman in America is a size 14. The funny side of me wants to ask, "So who wants to be below average?" and the more reasonable side of me asks, "If you are healthy and active, what difference does the number on the tag of your pants make?" But let's face it: When it comes to our bodies, circumnavigating all the messages we receive in our culture is not for the faint of heart. It's insanity, and, unless you live in a convent or cave with no television, magazines, newspapers, or billboards, it's in your face 24/7. I will never forget a comment I heard from a fashion designer several years ago. He said that the fashion industry is all about the clothes, not the people wearing the clothes, and the best way to highlight the clothes is to drape them over a "human hanger" rather than an actual person whose curves would interrupt the lines of the design. (!)

I bought a blouse the other day. It's hand beaded, striking, beautiful (and on sale!). But I was as taken by the message on the hanging tag as I was with the blouse. It reads: "I am your special garment. I am unique and often hand-woven, hand-beaded, hand-printed, and hand-painted. My defects are part of my beauty!!" If only we came with such a tag.

Even though some companies are trying to balance out the

messaging, it's hard to hear over the roar of the fashion industry at large. We get mixed messages from the media to "love" and take care of our bodies, yet most of us feel as if our bodies have betrayed us through some cruel metabolic joke, hormonal upheavals, and the effects of time and gravity. Therefore, the struggle to move from lamenting our bodies to accepting them may be monumental. Learning to *celebrate* our bodies is an even taller order.

Your body is a miracle; you know that, right? The fact that you have the organs and systems to keep everything running and cleaned out and oxygenated and balanced is nothing short of Divine Design. If you were to segment out just one minute of your existence, a mere sixty seconds, and have a biologist break down for you what happens in that single moment of respiration and cell rejuvenation alone, you would kiss your own toes (if you could reach them) and bless your very busy body for all it takes to keep you going from breath to breath. Because God has created you so uniquely and intricately, you are "Designer" no matter what label you wear on your clothes.

Still, we all know that body type, body reality, and body image aren't the same thing. Just ask anyone with anorexia nervosa. A female plagued with this eating disorder could be the size of a toothpick, have sunken eyes and her rib cage showing, but she says that when *she* looks in the mirror at herself all she sees is fat. This doesn't make sense to most of us from the outside looking in, but who lives their life from that vantage point? We live from the inside looking out, and because the mind is a curiously powerful messaging center, I would dare say that we all have a little bit of that kind of negative body fixation in us. When we look in the mirror, we naturally gravitate to our least attractive features. We wish we could change them or lose them or ignore them, but they just don't go away.

It's a complex issue, how we see ourselves and what our mind tells us about it. Sometimes we are seeing things that *aren't there* and other times we aren't seeing what *is there*. I have a theory that this is why we are perplexed whenever we see ourselves in photographs. Despite how bad we think we look, it seems our mental image is always better than what's portrayed in the photos, and when we see ourselves in a Kodak moment, we somehow can't believe that's really us. But then we also have the capability to obsess about certain parts of our bodies to the point of self-loathing when, in reality, it's not that bad.

Even Hollywood is starting to admit that this obsession is out of hand. I recently saw an author on an entertainment show discussing how Hollywood is embracing "normal-looking men" like Vince Vaughn and Jack Black, men with some girth. They even had a term for the normal-looking guys—"Flabulous." But the discussion quickly turned to the fact that there is no such designation for women in Hollywood, and no one seems to be embracing "normal-looking women." In fact, the host said you would never say that a girl was "flabulous." You would say she's out of shape.

I'm constantly reminded of this whole body-image thing being a gender-related problem as I watch my boys admire themselves in any mirror. They stand and stare with unabashed admiration.

They flex their biceps and admire them. They flex their triceps and admire them. They turn sideways and admire their physique from another angle. It's love, love, love in the mirror. By contrast, when any of the females in my household look in the mirror, we zoom in to the worst feature and linger there and walk away with a sigh. I routinely go to the grocery store in a ponytail and not a stitch of makeup, so I wouldn't consider myself overly concerned with my looks, but it is literally physically impossible for me to pass a mirror and not look at my midsection. (By "midsection" I am referring to everything from the top of my thighs to underneath my bra-line.) Why do I look at it every single time? Do I think that something mysteriously happened and it changed or shrank since the last time I looked at it ten minutes ago? Am I doing anything about it since I last looked at it? No, I'm just irrepressibly hopeful that this mirror might be the one that makes me seem less middle-heavy.

About the only time I ever looked at my middle with admiration was when I was with child. Ah, the good ol' days when you were eating for two and dressing for three or four. It used to be that when you were pregnant you had the luxury of wearing tent dresses for a while and not really worrying about your body shape for a nine-month reprieve period. No more, honey. Oh yes, the clothes now are a good deal cuter, but they are designed to show off your "bump" (notice the term even infers "little"—because when I was pregnant, it was definitely not a "bump," it was more like a "summit"). But now, you must be fashionably pregnant and your bump must be localized in the front and not migrate around to your backside. And by all means do not let your "bum" inherit any inches from your "bump"—or else you might not look cute in your hip maternity wardrobe.

If I sound a little messed up about this whole issue, it's probably latent bitterness over the INCREDIBLY HUGE tents we used to wear with big ol' white sailor collars, topped off with BIG RED BOWS. As if being big and uncomfortable weren't difficult enough, back in my pregnancy days the clothes were just hideous. But if the navy ever needed a parachute they could have borrowed any of my dresses. Occasionally a stiff wind would catch my billowing top and blow it up to the point that the middle "stretch panel" on my maternity pants was exposed. I recall being very embarrassed about that. If only I could have peered into the future to see a time when it would be chic to just let the whole pregnant belly hang out.

And I ask any female out there: How badly do the clothing manufacturers mess with our minds? You may *think* you know what size clothing you wear, but you may be wrong (at least part of the time). I recently read an article in a magazine about how sizes in America differ between brands and even between products in the same brand. The problem is there's no standard sizing guideline in the fashion industry. So a size six in one brand is a size zero in another. But every woman knows this fundamental truth: There is a size that is the top, the end of the earth, the point beyond which we believe there be dragons. This is The Size Above Which She Will Not Go. Should we get anywhere near it we will find a way to get consistent with the treadmill or Slim Fast until all pants button again. It's usually a temporary emergency (like January, for instance, or the month after a vacation). The top-of-the-wardrobe number varies from woman to woman, but we all have one firmly fixed in our minds.

At certain Levi's stores you can now go in and experience a machine called IntelliFit. Somewhat like the airport scanner machine, these use radio waves to get your precise measurements. You walk fully clothed into a booth and the machine ID's 200,000 points of measurement (who knew we had that many?), which are recorded and sent to a computer. Any computer that has that much info on any woman could easily qualify as The Beast. But instead of causing the end of the world, it spits out your precise dimension and prints out the sizes that will work best for you in that line of clothing. There is also a website called www.MyShape.com that doesn't use The Beast to get your measurements; it lets you do it at home with a good old tape measure. (Hopefully none of your measurements would end up posted on the Internet for the world to read.) But this website offers shopping services based on your measurements. What a relief for Hard-to-Fit. Even as I am writing this, I am personally thankful that the trend for the upcoming season is belts that fit directly below your bra line. Thank the Lord! They're finally putting belts where my waist *actually is.*

Almost every woman (if supplied with enough sodium pentothal) will tell you she wishes she looked like someone else. Which means that somewhere out there in your circle of acquaintances there's a woman wishing she looked like you. I call this the Beach Principle. If you go to any beach, you can always find someone smaller than you and someone larger than you. And females are always interested in knowing where they fall on the big/small scale. So we will ask whoever is seated next to us, be they friend or family member, "Tell me honestly—am I that big?" If they truly love you, they'll always answer no. If they're honest to a fault and happen to answer yes, that's the last time you'll ask for THEIR opinion.

Unfortunately, this penchant for comparison is a dangerous game. And it goes back to the very beginning of time. It seems that Satan was the highest cheese in the angelic pecking order, but it wasn't enough that he was the highest created being besides God Himself. He compared himself and didn't want just to be *like* God; the Bible tells us that he wanted to *be* God. You could almost bottom-line it and say that's what Satan got kicked out of heaven for: wanting to be someone else. So when we are in comparison mode, we are getting back to original sin (even before original sin), and quite frankly, Satan doesn't have too many more tricks besides this one. It's what he turned around and threw at Eve. ("You can be like God. You can know good from evil. Just like God. You want more, don't you? God doesn't want you to be like Him. Don't be content with how good you've got it right here. Compare and despair.") And his questioning worked. Eve, the woman who had it so good (think about it . . . walking and talk-ing with God, hanging out in the garden, having fun naked with her husband, no mother-in-law, no self-consciousness, no mirrors, and no one else to compare herself to), could not get past the fact that there might be something she was lacking. And in an instant, comparison became the mode of our daily lives.

Have you ever stopped to think how satisfied you might be with your own body if you weren't caught in the comparison trap for so many of your waking hours? Can you imagine how much more productive and available we could be if our hearts were untangled from that default mode? I challenge you (and me, too!) to pay close attention to your internal dialogue just for one day to see how often those kinds of thoughts invade your mind to make you feel "less than."

I read an interesting interview in *More* magazine (see? there's even a magazine called *More* to make us think that we might be missing out on something) a few months ago where they asked Susan Sarandon what it's like to be considered a sex siren at sixty years old. I know that seems like an oxymoron, but have you looked at the woman lately? It does give one cause for hope. While she still feels it's a kick for people to consider her in that way, she said that she feels more strongly than ever that she's got to work on herself on the inside "because you know the outside is a losing battle. It makes more sense to switch your focus to what kind of person you're becoming." Surprise, surprise. Paul told us this several hundred years ago, this principle of renewing ourselves inwardly because "outwardly we are wasting away" (2 Corinthians 4:16). As much as we would like to preserve our former youth and beauty, it's like trying to keep sand from slipping through an hourglass. Bodies morph with the changes of life. Is there a way as women we could ever move from our obsession with our less-than-perfect features toward a little more appreciation of all this miraculous vehicle allows us to do?

It seems to be more and more difficult to figure out if you are in The Healthy Zone than it used to be. Just a few years ago you could look at a little chart called "Height and Weight" to decide how you were doing physically. It was very straightforward: if you were _____ tall you should weigh between _____ and _____ pounds. In order to figure out your body mass index (the current standard used to let us know if we are too fat or too thin) you are forced to do a math project that is on the final exam for algebra majors. I am pasting in the calculation from the Wikipedia website because I don't even know what keystrokes one uses to type such an equation.

BMI is defined as the individual's body weight divided by the square of the height, and is almost always expressed in the unit kg/m², which is therefore often left out. The BMI value can be calculated with the following formulae.

SI units	Imperial Units
$BMI = \dfrac{weight \text{ (kg)}}{height^2 \text{ (m)}}$	$BMI = 703 \, \dfrac{weight \text{ (lb)}}{height^2 \text{ (in)}}$

"Simple formulae" — my foot!

When I went for my checkup a few weeks ago I had my "health care provider" (that's what they call them now — they aren't even doctors anymore) calculate my BMI for me. He pulled out a slide rule and had it figured out in less than fifteen seconds. It was awe inspiring. As for me, I have no idea what it is that the calculation above is asking for. And I want my height/weight chart back.

These days if you want to work on your body to be healthy and active we have more options than ever. I am amazed just at the number of health and fitness programs on infomercials late at night. There's that guy with the really long blonde ponytail sticking out of his baseball cap with his machine that is supposed to simulate "natural walking motion." Is that really something we need to simulate? I hate to be Captain Obvious here, but why not just WALK? Hello! If you just flip through basic cable between the hours of midnight and 6 a.m. you can find various Pilates instructional videos, an incredible array of bizarre equipment, and even something called a "yoga booty ballet." I wasn't aware that one could attain a "yoga booty." If you have one, please let me know so I can know if I need one of those.

Have you ever thought about the fact that the whole subject of exercise is basically a new invention? You can hardly find anything written about it before 1940. Back then exercise was called "life." You had lots of movement associated with getting from 7 a.m. to 10 p.m. and, in the course of going about your daily business, you happened to burn a lot of calories getting from point A to point B, doing things that no one had invented machines to do yet. And have you seen the people who were considered "body builders" back in the forties and fifties? No steroid enhancement there, just lots of beef. And nobody sat around inventing things like the ThighMaster back then. They were trying to master other things like electricity, gas-powered engines, telephones, and television—you know, all those things that now keep us from getting exercise. Of course, I guess you'd have to take into account the historical accounts of those ancient Greek goofballs who thought up the Olympics, but they competed naked. Eeeeew. No athletic apparel endorsements there.

I went to Curves for a while and I really enjoyed it (ok, so "enjoyed" it might be a slight stretch, but it's very easy for us ADHD types because you only spend a few seconds on each type of equipment before the voice from up above tells you to "Now change stations," so you don't have time to get bored). It didn't really work for me because I travel so much. (I know they have locations in other towns, but never in the area where my hotel is located.) But the reason I used to love to go to Curves was to listen to the women talk to each other as they made their rounds. It was hilarious to listen to these women who were there specifically to work out and lose weight—and what, pray tell, do they talk about the whole time they're there? Food! Recipes! And not just the ones modified for diet, but all kinds of fabulous recipes for food. And as they were wiping their faces off with their little exercise towelettes, I would hear them exchange e-mail addresses and promise to e-mail the recipes as soon as they got home. You just can't trump human nature. After awhile I decided it probably was counterproductive to go because I was too hungry from listening to them describe the food. But my favorite Curves location has to be the one in Destin, Florida. It is in a strip mall next to a Dippin' Dots ice cream shop. Talk about motivation to go every day!

I read online that eating whatever you want when you want to and not gaining any weight is a matter of psychology. Basically it's all in our heads (and we thought it was in our derrieres). Women who accept their bodies and eat whenever they're hungry and stop whenever they're full weighed less than women who obsessed about their weight. Well, duh. If I weighed less to begin with I wouldn't be obsessed about my weight either. But I know what they're trying to say. If we are constantly thinking about what we cannot have, it plays into our lowest nature to then want THAT VERY THING we are trying to avoid. It's like saying, "Whatever you do, don't think about polka-dotted elephants." At that moment—even if you never had any intention of ever thinking about polka-dotted elephants—you find yourself unable to think of anything else. So when your diet plan says, "absolutely no chocolate," you find yourself unable to stop thinking about how soon you could lay your hands on just one bite. The Polka-Dotted Elephant Syndrome strikes again.

But wait . . . as women, is our worth really determined by the number staring back at us on the bathroom scale? We can change our bodies somewhat through exercise and elective surgery, but the genetic code we were dealt cannot be undone. Depending on who's up your family tree, your tendency to carry weight in your thighs like your dad or to have an allergic reaction to seafood like your mom just can't be controlled or eliminated. Every morning we still have to face the mirror and figure out how to get past the self-condemnation that creeps into our minds every time we glance at a *Cosmo* cover in the grocery store line.

I have a better idea. Actually, it came from Tyra Banks. On her talk show I recently watched a segment called "Fix It or Flaunt It." Tyra found people on the street, asked them what their flaws or problems were, and right there on the spot declared that she didn't know if it should be fixed or flaunted. She had her team of stylists work on each girl and as they came back on camera to reveal their new look, the audience was astonished that several of the girls were now "flaunting" their formally most unattractive feature. One girl had a very high forehead. When I say very high, think "billboard." They didn't cut some bangs to hide it, they actually pulled the hair high up into a barrette, curled all the hair coming down the side, and made a monument to that forehead. And it worked. The chick looked positively chic.

So, what a great concept: If you can't fix it, accentuate it! Go all the way with it. Instead of denying the feature you're not enamored with, maybe you should put it all the way out there and make it your signature. Or, if that's just too much of a stretch for you, you could at least try adopting this philosophy, loosely quoted and oft attributed to professional motorcycle racer Bill McKenna: "Life is not a journey to the grave with the intention of arriving safely in one pretty and well preserved piece, but to skid across the line broadside, thoroughly used up, worn out, leaking oil, shouting GERONIMO!"

if money grew on trees, we'd all be staunch ecologists

Traditional wisdom (the kind you can get in Proverbs or perhaps a Beatles song) informs us that "money can't buy you love." And they'll also tell you that money can't buy you happiness. But I've had money and I've had no money, and I can tell you from experience that money can, indeed, buy you a better brand of misery.

There is a universal truth that some people are just going to have more money than others, so it is up to us to decide if we are going to get a number and join the marathon called The Rat Race (more money, more stuff, more money to pay for more stuff, a larger place to keep all the stuff and the money, more people to help us make and take care of the stuff and the money, more worry about losing our stuff and our money) or if we are going to sit it out, wear Birkenstocks, and eat granola.

I'll just come right out and say it: I like stuff. This doesn't seem very spiritual, but it's true. I especially like gadgets. I'm intrigued by little pieces of technology that hold forth the promise of doing things more efficiently. We recently got a one-cup-at-a-time brewing machine because we didn't all want the same coffee or tea at the same time. It's somewhat like an iPod for hot beverage drinkers. I rationalized that it was great stewardship because we wouldn't be pouring out half a carafe of unused coffee every day, but I think I really just like the idea of having a cup of Earl Grey tea all to myself in less than thirty seconds.

This is madness, I know. If I were financially able (and had already given all that I could in tithes, offerings, and special missions projects) and I had even *more* extra money lying around, I have to admit that I would probably get one of everything in Brookstone, Sharper Image, AND Hammacher-Schlemmler. I would. That's how much I enjoy goofy gadgets. Last summer we ordered the Wind Chill fan—this is an outdoor fan that hooks up to our garden hose and sprays a mist as it blows, like the ones they use at the summer Olympics and at theme parks. It cools the air temp down by about twenty degrees so that, as I am lying out in the sun, I don't actually have to suffer any of the effects of the heat. Cool, literally.

But no matter how many gadgets I could ever amass I am painfully aware that Bill Gates would have more and cooler gadgets than I. This is because he is the richest man ever (or is it Warren Buffet? I forget). But Bill Gates and all his money can't buy a good haircut. Come to think of it, neither can Donald Trump. I see a trend. Maybe it's another way that God equals things out. Big money = bad hair. I *can* guarantee you that I will never have a haircut that bad because I will *never* have as much money as them.

This is because I do not understand *anything* about how finances/ economy/money work. Oh, I get the basics: I need to exchange my dollars for goods and services, but beyond that, I cannot figure out the system.

I go to the bank. I put money in. Somehow the money goes away very quickly. I know that I am responsible for this, but the outgo does have a head start on the inflow, having been sitting around for at least twenty-four hours and itching to get out into the world. I suspect that whenever new, energetic money comes in, the old money bolts, frequently knocking some of the new money back out the door along with it. Whatever the mystery, the money shuffle messes with my bank account statements. I long ago gave up trying to balance my checkbook. I do get that the input should exceed the output, but I don't understand why it falls to me to have to make sure that the statement is exactly right. (They're the bank, right? Isn't it *their job* to figure that out?) So I just go online, look at the number they have as my ending balance, and imagine the difference between the money I put in this month versus the amount of checks I think I wrote this month. If the number they say I have and the number I think I should have are less than $25 apart, I go with their number. It's bad accounting, but it saves me a lot of time. I could sit there for countless hours looking for $25, or just pay myself $25 not to care. My sanity is worth $25, and if time is money, I just saved myself a lot of both.

Stock market? I don't get that either. I get that you buy "stock" in a certain "market" and then you're supposed to leave it there for a very long time to make more money than you could acquire through interest on a savings account. The place where all of this happens is called "Wall Street," meaning that there is a "wall" that divides the Stock Market Savvy people and the rest of the yokels. This place is inhabited by "brokers," obviously derived from the fact that, with a single bad day of trading, you could be very "broke." They trade on something called the NASDAQ, which sounds like a rogue racing circuit or a rap group. You can actually buy stock in something called "futures" of pork bellies. (Why would I want a pig's innards now, much less in the future?) Seems like "playing" the stock market is basically a legalized form of gambling combined with Psychic Friends Network. I am going to vote "No" on that. I have also heard of studies that have shown that chickens pecking to choose stocks and monkeys who choose stocks often do as well as financial advisors. If I ever invest in the stock market I'll consult with the animals and save trader fees.

There is also something called the Federal Reserve Board, and it has a chairman. This man is charged with the responsibility of raising and lowering something called the prime rate, which, according to Google (the definitive source for all accurate financial information), is "the lowest rate of interest on bank loans at a given time and place, offered to preferred borrowers." I don't know how you get on the "preferred borrowers" list, but I'm pretty sure my name is not on it. In emotional terms, the Female Prime Interest Rate is better defined by how *interested* we are in a given subject. For instance:

Fox South Sports Report: Female Prime Interest Rate is 1 percent and cooling.

Fashion Report on the Red Carpet of the Oscars: Female Prime Interest Rate is 33 percent and steady.

Clearance Sale on the Shoe Rack at Nordstroms: Female Prime Interest Rate is 87 percent and climbing fast.

It's not that I haven't tried to understand the wide world of economics. I took economics in college, and though I made a B on my report card, I can say unequivocally that I haven't a clue about how a national economy works. It has something to do with supply and demand (which I've experienced with certain coveted toys at Christmas time). Other than that, my uncle explained it best. He espoused his Cookie Sheet Full of Water Theory of Politics and Economics at our last family reunion.

My Uncle John told me (well, he didn't exactly tell *me*, he was talking with one of my boy cousins and I happened to overhear the conversation) that every time a president gets elected, the country hands him the economy. This economy is the equivalent of a cookie sheet filled with water. He explained that the president is in charge of carrying that very shallow pan full of water from the day he gets into office until the day he leaves office without it tipping a little to the left or the right and letting all the water run out. If you've never tried to carry a cookie sheet full of water from one side of a room to another you ought to go to your kitchen and try it.

I'll wait.

Did you go?

How are you ever going to know what it feels like to be in charge of a national economy?

Okay, then, I see your level of commitment to understanding economics. It's the same as mine.

Other people must have the same disconnect to financial terminology as myself. We have television shows with very earnest people telling us how to manage our money and how to understand economic issues. I've watched Suze Orman on TV as she has tried to explain to us lesser mortals the many intricacies of finances. I do not understand why this woman is so excitable, but her very large teeth disturb me. You can see about 80 percent of the teeth that occupy her mouth and you simply cannot concentrate while viewing that much enamel. And the more excited she gets about someone's financial issue, it seems that she gnashes them while telling people to not be stupid with their money. This does not comfort me, so I don't stay with her show very long. Plus, her production team sends graphics flying in on the screen with whooshing sound effects to reinforce whatever she just said through her large teeth. These graphics have bullet points that always say the same things:

- Write down every penny you make and every penny you spend.
- Find any areas that look like you may enjoy them.
- Stop doing those things immediately, if not sooner.
- And stop looking at my teeth.

It can make you feel mucho insecure about your ability to manage your own finances, but never fear! Every day there are hundreds of people entering the marketplace with the title of

"Financial Planner." These are people who have studied finances and equations and options to help you reach your financial goals *by selling you life insurance and taking a percentage of your money.* This does not make sense to me. Why can't we just *keep* our money instead of giving it to them so they can tell us how to make it? That's like a Jack and the Beanstalk approach. And they tell us we need to buy more and more life insurance—*their* life insurance. They give us choices like "term life" versus "whole life" (I would prefer to live my "whole life" on my own "terms," if you don't mind). And these financial planners recommend books with titles like *The Millionaire Next Door*. I heard this author discussing his book on the radio, and his whole concept in a nutshell is "pay yourself first." Right. So then would I really dun myself if I didn't pay myself first? Would I leave threatening messages on my own voice mail saying I would repossess my own car?

Financial planners will also help you figure out how much you will need for retirement. They will have the normal categories, like housing, health care, utilities, and food. But they don't cover all the bases, like these necessary line items:

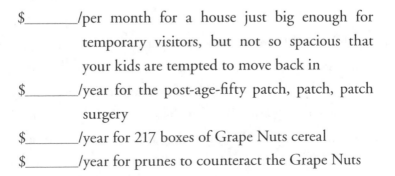

$_____/per month for a house just big enough for temporary visitors, but not so spacious that your kids are tempted to move back in

$_____/year for the post-age-fifty patch, patch, patch surgery

$_____/year for 217 boxes of Grape Nuts cereal

$_____/year for prunes to counteract the Grape Nuts

And with the teetering status of our Social Security program, you may have to work until you're eighty just to get by. I know this because I get those statements once a year that say, based upon my current amount of contributions, I would get $212 per month should I choose to retire at 65. That would not even cover the Grape Nuts. (Discuss: neither a Grape nor a Nut.)

Wouldn't it be nice if the educational system would just give us some financial training in elementary school so we wouldn't have to learn the concepts the hard way? But considering what they've done with sex education, maybe we should be glad that they are leaving finances alone. We get most of our financial training by observation of our own parents (mixed bag), our friends (probably no more mature than we are), and later our colleagues and a variety of associates. We try a little of this, we try a little of that. And we somehow imagine that other people know more than we do about how to manage money. The sad truth is that most of us are just making it up as we go along.

And all of us have money "personalities" to go along with our half-baked ideas about money management. Take the Saver and the Spender. Normally in a marriage there will be one of each, which could explain why many divorces are precipitated over money. John and I are not opposites, per se, but we have different ideas of what constitutes a comfortable margin in our finances.

Each of my kids has a unique approach to finances. We call Calvin, my oldest, "Dollar Boy." He has some, hardly ever spends it (his standard defense: "I left my wallet at home"), so what little he has lasts a *long* time. He got the name Dollar Boy because that's the only amount he would ever put in gasoline in his truck. We tried to convince him that putting twenty dollars' worth in his tank once was the same as putting one dollar's worth in twenty times. Not in his mind. Austin, our middle child, we call "Mr. Spends for da Friends." He makes some, spends a lot, and can run through whatever he has without batting an eyelash. But he enjoys it while he has it. If he can ever get the same joy out of saving as he gets out of spending, it'll eventually even out. Baby Girl Elyse is well known for her deep need for super-wide margins in her life. Therefore, she makes a lot, spends a little, and saves a lot. The boys protest that this is because Daddy gets her whatever she wants. This is partially true. For her, the bigger the balance in her savings account, the bigger the smile on her face. She may be the only one of my children who will be able to afford to take care of me in my old age.

One thing that's true of all our kids, however, is that they are *givers*, mainly because our church has taught them to really *celebrate* giving. Every Sunday our whole congregation reads aloud together verses from the Old and New Testament that talk about the joy of giving and God's promises associated with giving. And in our church we march our offering up to the front. People can't just "stealth give" as the plate comes past them. In our church we also pray every Sunday for those in our congregation who are unemployed or underemployed (I think that may be a little more subjective, but whatever). It is a wonderful reminder of the fact that having the health and ability to earn money is a privilege, as is giving it away.

Daniel Gilbert, a Harvard psychology professor and author

of *Stumbling on Happiness*, contends that beyond a certain point money has very little to do with happiness. He says that the happiness we derive from any financial gain is what we get from our money divided by what our neighbors make (or, more accurately, what we perceive they are making). Once again, it comes back to the comparison issue. Two Princeton professors, economist Alan B. Krueger and psychologist Daniel Kahneman, collaborated with colleagues from three other universities on a study that confirmed that the widespread belief that high income is associated with a sense of well-being is mostly illusory. "People with above-average income are relatively satisfied with their lives but are barely happier than others in moment-to-moment experience, tend to be more tense, and do not spend more time in particularly enjoyable activities," the researchers reported.

Also, consider the words of Bruce Weinstein, the author of *Life Principles: Feeling Good by Doing Good*: "Beyond a certain point, more money does not equate with more happiness. If it did, you would expect to find the wealthiest or most famous people to be the happiest, and that is simply not the case. Once our basic needs are met, it turns out that it's friendship and being loved and having someone to love that makes life worth living."

So how do you consider yourself? Happy and poor? Miserable and rich? Miserable and poor? Happily wealthy? The truth is that no matter where you fall on the economic ladder, if you have a roof over your head and you ate twice today, you are far wealthier than 90 percent of the rest of the world. Once again it comes back to attitude.

Our pastor recently gave a message on poverty mentality versus abundance mentality. He asked us how we feel about whatever it is that we have. Do we hold it with an open hand and share and give and believe that there will always be more? Or do we hoard, afraid that there won't be enough tomorrow? Jesus spoke of this when discussing the widow's mite with His disciples. He said, "The truth is that this poor widow gave more to the collection than all the others put together. All the others gave what they'll never miss; she gave extravagantly what she couldn't afford—she gave her all" (Mark 12:43-44, MSG). Her gift exhibited a spirit of abundance (seems ironic) in that she believed that the God who provided for her needs would be able to provide again. Like the Doritos commercial, "Don't worry. We'll make more."

John and I both recognize elements of poverty mentality in our personalities, and we've been trying to address them. In the end it really has to do with our faith in God's ability to provide for us. John has more of a tendency to save things; it started when he was little. He wouldn't allow anyone to eat his birthday cake. He would save it until it molded. No one got to eat it, but he got to look at it for a long time. I have the spirit of "I want to make it last" manifested in another way: Let me purchase multiples of this thing I need just in case I don't have enough money to purchase it again. Where does this spirit of lack come from inside of us? Neither of us grew up deprived or destitute, yet we recognize this inability to trust God with our stuff.

I think a question many of us need to ask ourselves is, What are we saving for? And what is driving our saving? Is it love or is it fear? And what is our definition of "enough"? We may not think that we have a lot. But if we could imagine what we do have being lost in a fire and then being told the next morning that it was all a bad dream and we suddenly had it all back, wouldn't we think we were the richest women in the world? Clearly, the issue isn't so much about what we have, but what we *think* of what we have.

A recent *Time* magazine cover story titled, "Does God Want You to Be Rich?" discussed the various theological stands regarding wealth, from one end of the continuum of "blessed are the poor" to the polar opposite approach of "blessed to be a blessing." Interestingly enough there were equal amounts of Scripture to support both stances. Jesus spoke more about money, wealth, the problems associated with money (usually from having so much that you forget the source of the wealth), how to give it (cheerfully) and save it (like the ants), and how to make more in your endeavors (by investing rather than hoarding) than He did about the existence of heaven or hell. I think this is incredibly interesting of Jesus to camp on the subject matter that reveals our true feelings about God's provision, His sovereignty, the abilities He's gifted us with by which we make a living, the virtue of generosity, and what makes life worth living.

So what does money represent for you? Security? Stability? The ability to provide for your family? Power? A hedge against hard times? You can choose to do things to make more money and acquire more things, but short of winning the lottery, the Joneses are always going to keep that carrot a little ahead of your nose. How do you decide when enough is enough? In her book *Your*

Money or Your Life, Vicki Robin talks about not making a living but "making a dying." Her idea is that we continue to work harder and harder to make more money to spend on more things, which requires us to make more money. As a result we have become financially wealthy and time poor.

Whether you are barely getting by, just getting along, starting to get ahead, or getting rich, you can view your financial status in a way where "getting" is not the primary goal of your life. You can't take it with you, but you can do a lot of good with what you're entrusted with while you're here. Your money or your life, indeed. If time is money, and time is life, you can literally exchange one for the other. Choose carefully.

if you can't beat 'em, tickle 'em

It sounds like a bet he might have lost in a dart game, but there is a man who *voluntarily* read the entire *Encyclopedia Britannica* and lived to tell about it. His name is A. J. Jacobs and he wrote a book about his experience called *The Know-It-All: One Man's Humble Quest to Become the Smartest Person in the World.* Not that I haven't been tempted to try it when I was younger. (We had a set and I loved to look at the pictures of bizarre skin diseases and illustrations of the human reproductive system — and it was filled with such pronouncements as, "One day our government hopes to send a man to the moon.") But I now possess the knowledge that I can't retain much besides my Social Security number and ankle fluid. The memorization of random (though alphabetical) facts would be useless if I couldn't use my compendium of knowledge to impress people. I would be stuck saying things like, "Oh, I remember reading something about that . . ." and trailing off as I send my mental secretary to fetch that file, only to find that she is on permanent coffee break.

In college I did attempt to commit large segments of my constitutional development textbook to memory. This was back when I thought I was going to law school and would need this information at my mental beck and call in my pursuit of better jurisprudence. I could regurgitate all sorts of Somebody vs. Someone Else and how this decision affected constitutional law. I wrote the cases on index cards, memorized them, discussed them with other law-minded students, raised my hand, and got class participation points for knowing them at the right moment. I wrote a lot about them in the standard issue college blue books and even debated them on the debate team as we competed against other college teams over the subject matter of the "penumbra rights to privacy." Today, if you held a gun to my head and asked me to bring even *one* of them back from the murky waters of my memory, you'd just have to shoot me. So much for "knowing" something.

And, of course, I didn't become a lawyer. Not that I couldn't have, it's just that when I got my undergraduate degree I couldn't figure out which sort of practice of law would interest me. I didn't want to do civil law (divorces and wills, bo-ring), criminal law (defending guilty people or fighting toe-to-toe with those who did), corporate law (exchanging loopholes for $$$), environmental nor entertainment law (tree hugging or high-maintenance clients), so the point of my college education seemed to be that I found out that I didn't want to do what I thought I wanted to do.

We have often heard it said, "It's not what you know, it's who you know." But if you ask any fifteen-year-old trying to pass the written part of the driver's test or a seventeen-year-old nervously drumming a pencil as he stares down at an SAT test, he would tell you that is pure baloney. In that moment, no one is interested in whether or not your dad is friends with the governor. You have to show *what* you know. Your privilege to drive or your college acceptance is riding on your ability to recall the right answers. And there are many of us who just don't test well. We know the information and we could regurgitate it under any other circumstance, but put a bunch of questions with multiple choice empty circles to fill in with a #2 lead pencil and our brains turn to jelly. For some an exam is a chance to prove their mental prowess, for others it induces sheer terror. But whether you have feelings of inferiority or superiority, exams don't accurately reflect what you *do* with what you know anyway. And what you do with what you know is the only measure of education that truly matters, in my humble opinion.

What is intelligence? Your score on an IQ test? I don't think I've ever been evaluated for that. If I was, perhaps they opted not to share the sad number with me for fear that it would damage my widdle psyche. Is intelligence an ability to memorize facts and recall them? Or is it the ability to solve problems? Is it a direct reflection of how many years of schooling you have? The concept of "educated fools" can be witnessed on C-SPAN any day of the year. Is it even possible to measure *real* intelligence? Maybe it's just the good sense to get out of the rain.

Marilyn von Savant (could that really be her real name?) is supposedly the smartest woman in the world. She has the highest recorded IQ (228) and is married to the Dr. Robert Jarvik who invented the Jarvik 7 artificial heart—so at least she was smart enough to snag a doctor. And wouldn't you like to eavesdrop on their breakfast conversations! She writes the mental challenge column in *Parade Magazine* every Sunday. It's called "Ask Marilyn." (I said she was intelligent, not creative.) But hey, don't knock it. She has figured out a way to work one day a week and she doesn't even have to write half a column. People do it for her. I say she must be pretty smart based on that fact alone! She dishes out little conundrums or solves little problems people send in, like, "Can you change one letter of each of these words to make all new words?" She answers such queries as (this is an actual question sent in to her—I am not making this up), "My wife and I won entry into a drawing for a $10,000 prize. In all, 13 families who'd won entry arrived at the drawing. So 13 keys—one of which would open the gate to the grand prize—were placed in a basket, and the families lined up. We believe the last family in line had the best chance, and we were in 11th position, yet the prize was won by the family in 10th position. We never had a chance to draw a key. Which position do you think had the best chance?" (By the way, the answer was that all positions were equal.) Are you totally kidding me? Who has time to think this stuff up? In the case of the question about the keys, I can tell you that one was sent in by a middle child—they are the world's Guardians of Fairness. So this is what Mensas sit around and talk about. Must make for fascinating (yawn) conversations.

I have heard that a large number of the people who are members of Mensa are basically unemployable because they are too smart.

Can you imagine? This proves that too much of a good thing can sometimes just be too much. Perhaps it also explains why they can't concentrate on their work—because they are busy thinking up questions to try to stump their Queen Mensa. None of the rest of us has time to explore the unused 90 percent of our brains with hypothetical situations or word problems when we're trying to figure out how to get the disposal unstuck or the English pea out of our four-year-old's nose. Why don't they print the answers to *those* questions in a Sunday paper?

Maybe we should start a column for people whose IQ is less than half of Marilyn's and teach her the stuff *we* know, like:

- You can mix up deviled egg filling in a baggie, snip the end off to fill the whites, then throw the bag away without messing up a spoon or bowl (now *that's* smart!).
- Windex or hairspray will kill insects and ants in a pinch.
- If you pin a safety pin to the bottom of your half slip, you won't get static cling (really!).
- If you leave a tooth in cola for three days it will disappear. (So don't set your glass of Coke next to Granddaddy's denture cup.)

Take that, Mensas!

IQ scores also cannot measure good old-fashioned wisdom (good sense coupled with experience). My mom has always lamented the fact that she didn't go to college, but she is such a great observer of people and is a dedicated reader, so I would say that makes her a scholar in her own right. She has cultivated the admirable quality of being a lifelong learner. Perhaps I should frame a diploma for her: "Advanced Studies of Modern Civilization and Comparative Fiction." That sounds very official.

I am grateful to live in an age when ignorance is purely elective. If we desire to know something badly enough, we can know it. Endless streams of specific knowledge about very detailed subject matters that used to be exclusive to academia are now freely accessible on the Internet. It is entirely possible that a person can become an "expert" in a matter of weeks, should they so choose.

Conversely, everyone is ignorant about something. This may be one of the great gifts of aging—the knowledge that there is so much you will probably never know. It can spur you on to more mental exploration, frustrate you to the point of giving up, or cause you to appreciate your friends and acquaintances who are experts in areas you know little about. You don't have to know it all. In fact, you can't. And even brilliant people can miss the honor roll from time to time. According to some accounts of his early learning, even Einstein was no "Einstein" in the classroom.

But I loved the classroom. I don't know if I had a slight addiction to chalk dust or the corrugated cardboard that lined the bulletin boards, but I always loved school. I fell in love with the classroom on day one of kindergarten, where my teacher told my mom to make sure that I never had a chance to get bored in first grade. I always assumed it was a compliment on my superior intelligence until it dawned on me that she was possibly commenting on my ability to get into trouble when I was not focused. I loved school so much that I would actually fake being well when I was febrile so that my mom wouldn't make me stay home. This doesn't make sense to anyone who ever tried to stay home by faking a fever, but I was bound and determined to board that yellow bus every morning.

In high school I was a good student, but not what you would call "outstanding" in the usual categories. Not brainy enough to be in National Honor Society. Not public-service-minded enough to be in the Key Club. Not athletic enough to letter. Not popular enough to run for student body president. I worked on yearbook and was a star member of the Future Business Leaders of America. I even went to the state level competition for the venerable FBLA. It's too bad I can't tell you anything about business principles now. Apparently that was unretainable knowledge.

If only I had known that you had to work on the yearbook EVERY year (hence the name "*year*book"). This is one of those secrets they never tell you when you enter high school: that if you work on the yearbook just *one* year, you're not considered quite loyal enough to get the recognition on senior awards day. But I'm over it. Really. (I hope you're reading this, Miss Futyma.)

Where I found I could excel was on a stage. I was talented in the "entertainment" area, and that made my myriad inadequacies bearable. When I was in elementary school I was entered in a couple of those local beauty contest things. It was innocent enough in my little hometown, pretty much just an excuse to dress up and show off your kid. The only problem was that I was . . . how shall we say? Okay, I was chubby. There was not a snowball's chance that I would be in serious contention for the beauty trophy. But baby, let me tell you, I could sing and play the piano *simultaneously*. Don't think *that* didn't trump the baton twirlers! I used to sing and play the Burt Bacharach song "I'll Never Fall in Love Again." I realize the irony of a plump ten-year-old singing those lyrics, but how cute was I when I sang, "What do you get when you kiss a guy? You get enough germs to catch pneumonia" and inserted my own little sneeze? You think the judges didn't make up their minds right then and there? I got the talent trophy every time. Which is good, because I never got the Little Miss Whatever sash. (When the promoters of the big beauty pageants say, "It's all about the scholarships," I always think, *Who are they kidding?* If these girls and their families took all the money they spent on pageant gowns, makeup, hair, personal trainers, travel expenses, and vocal coaching, they could have paid their own way to college and then they wouldn't need a "scholarship." It's about the tiara, baby! Girls want the tiara and the sash and the title and the undeniable bragging rights that go with the term "queen.")

In the summer between my junior and senior years of high school I was chosen to participate in the Fredericksburg Summer Stock Theater, where *real* actors and actresses (from New York City — how urbane!) would come in for the season and fill in with local bit part players. I auditioned and got the part of Princess #2 in the musical *The Princess and the Pea* because I could sing and I had long legs. You cannot possibly imagine how far out of my box this whole experience was for me. Having grown up Baptist and unathletic I was never picked for *anything* on the basis of my legs, as I was not allowed to show them. Ever. For any reason. But my parents allowed me to be a part of those shows because they believed that it would help me develop the talents God gave me.

Sometimes we get to thinking that life is a pageant and we have to win in at least one category, so we apply the Pageant Logic: If you're not so good-looking, surely you could win the talent portion. If you're not talented, maybe you're congenial. We consider people like Barbara Streisand, who by her own admission is not considered to be a classic beauty, to be enormously successful because of her singing and acting abilities. Some are not talented but smart—others are not smart or talented, but have amazing beauty, sometimes only on the inside. Perhaps their talents are not obvious and you might not be able to identify them even if you saw them in action. They are subtle. They don't require a microphone or a spotlight.

I have no idea what your educational background is, but I do know that education is not The End All of Life. You could be the most intelligent person in the world in the realm of facts, but if you have no interest in people you'd miss out on the sweetness of life. You may not have graduated from high school but may possess a heart of brilliant wisdom.

We can't change IQ or lengthen our list of natural talents, but all of us can continue to learn throughout our lives and use the talents we do have to bless the people within our reach. We are all gifted in our own right, and it is a spiritual tenet that we are to have a sane evaluation of our gifts and intelligence. Overestimate and we stumble into pride. Underestimate and we cheat ourselves out of opportunities because we fail to see ourselves in that role. Only we can rightly value the gifts God has placed inside us and use them to honor Him.

There are a couple of universal truths that apply no matter what your education, your IQ, or your list of talents. You have the choice every day for the rest of your life to focus on what you *do have* and what you *can do* or what you don't have and what you can't do. The apostle Paul would have never given us the instruction to intentionally focus on things that are true, lovely, admirable, etc., if he didn't mean for us to choose what to think about. So value your own intelligence. Own your mental real estate. Celebrate your areas of expertise and revel in your unique talents. Continue to learn your whole life long. We aren't competing in a pageant or proving our IQ on a piece of paper. Don't worry about how you can "beat 'em"—just be your best at whatever God has intentionally made you to be.

if blood is **thicker** than water, **one** is much better for swimming

Around 1990, shortly after the dawn of equal access long distance telephone service, one of the large telecommunications companies pulled what appeared to be a marketing coup with the introduction of the Friends & Family calling program. It offered a lower rate for calls made to people that a customer had designated in their "calling circle." These folks had to be customers of the company, too. If any customer decided to take up with a competitor that offered a better deal, they would have to explain to their "friends and family" that calling them would now cost more. It was a great idea to encourage customer loyalty, but as competition heated up, people became reluctant to fuss with determining who could call who for a reduced price, and eventually the whole plan was scrapped.

Nowadays we have various knockoffs in the cellular phone industry. If you can get your friends and family to sign up for service with the same provider as you, you will get to talk to each other without using up any of your minutes. It seems like a good idea, but if you have ever tried to get your friends or family to even switch *sodas* you might have a clue that this can be a hard sell. Besides, do you really want to have to talk with your mother — much less your cousin in Alabama — for an *unlimited time*?

Your family is sorta like your body — you get what you get and you get to do with it what you can. Friends? Sometimes you pick them, sometimes they pick you. I love the movie *Beaches* because it shows a friendship over the course of time in which people grow and change, life situations alter, geography gets in the way, but the friendship survives even in death. True friends are like the family you wish you'd had, and I've heard it said that friends are God's way of apologizing for your family. No matter what you think of either, your association with your family and friends will fundamentally change you.

It's important that we have friends who are different from us, otherwise the friendship can be boring, and let's be honest, we have *nothing* to learn from someone who's exactly like us. Researchers have found that having good friends can increase longevity, relieve anxiety, and lower blood pressure. I'm supposing that the opposite is true of a "bad" friend. In fact, you may someday soon be able to get a note from your doctor to give to your "bad" friend stating that you can "no longer be friends for medical reasons."

According to a study published by *The Lancet Neurology*, people with large social circles often score higher on tests and stave off dementia longer. Researchers have no idea why but speculate that maintaining friendships helps build new neural pathways in your brain. So it's officially medically proven: friends make you smarter. Any woman knows this is true because the web of knowledge that is weaved through a single conversation between more than two friends greatly expands your personal knowledge base (not just facts and figures, but, you know, real human interest stories!). So, if a highly respected journal in medicine says that getting together with friends makes you smarter, then there's just another reason to plan the next girls' night out. When anyone asks you where you're going, tell them it's a little-known branch of Mensa.

The term "friend" may not carry the weight that it has in centuries past with the advent of MySpace, Facebook, and Xanga. These are websites where you can get some "friends" via the Internet. Though these web pages seem like they're mostly for teenagers, while surfing MySpace.com I noticed that C. S. Lewis has his own page. So obviously you don't even have to be *alive* to have one. On a MySpace page you can upload information about yourself and a few favorite photos, and invite people *you already know* to come and be your friend. (Well, how much sense does that make? They're already your friends or you wouldn't be able to invite them . . . duh.) They can come and leave comments about you and then other random people who are friends of your friends can post on your page that they would like to be your friend, too, only *now* you have to decide if they are worthy of your friendship based on their MySpace page and whether or not you want to open yourself up to their ilk of friends. If you don't like the way their MySpace page looks, you can *deny* their friendship. How powerful! Not only that, but you can rate your friends by moving their pictures closer to the top of your list. This sort of tells your friends where they fall in the pecking order. Do not venture into the world of MySpace if you have thin skin because you are going to get denied, my friend. It's the Internet version of seventh grade, only less subtle. The object is to network with as many friends of friends as you can amass, but it also reminds me of the cardinal party maxim: A friend of a friend may come to a party but the friend of friend may not invite *their* friends to the party. The MySpace world of "friendship" is not really friendship at all. It's just a cyberspace connection.

The truth is that true friendship = risk. That's the only thing about relationships that is absolutely certain. Whenever you extend yourself in relationship, you extend yourself in risk. For those who don't handle risk well, the prospect of relationship is always difficult. You are sharing a degree of intimacy and information that you must now entrust to another's ability to keep a confidence. It is possible that you may end up with emotional "burn wounds" from a prior friendship in which you allowed people who were not trustworthy inside your confidence and later regretted it. But alongside these risks is the possibility for rich emotional rewards that only camaraderie and shared life experience can afford.

Once in a while your friend will disappoint you. I had a certain friend when my children were young. Our kids were close in age, and our friendship was based on a lot of activities that happened concurrently at the church as both our husbands were on staff there. Being as young and idealistic as I was, I assumed a certain

measure of commitment in the relationship (and here's the problem) based on *my* view of how friendship "should" be. One day
John had to take our only car to a meeting a couple of hours away.
My friend and I were going to the same Bible study group that
morning, so I called and asked her if she could come by and pick
me up on the way. Simple enough—not really much out of her
way, something I would have done for her. My friend (who was
a nurse by trade and very structured) replied that she could not
because she had planned to go to the craft store on the way to the
Bible study, and if she waited until *after* the Bible study, her little
girl would be fifteen minutes behind schedule for her nap. I recall
the tears stinging in my eyes as I hung up, feeling like a very low
priority on her scale. It took me several days to figure out that my
hurt wasn't as much rooted in the rejection of the ride as it was in
figuring out that *my* definition of friendship (flexibility, loyalty,
availability) wasn't the same thing as *her* definition of friendship. When I realized that her personality traits of orderliness and
efficiency were things that made her great in her profession (see
chapter 6, again!), it made more sense to me. We didn't lose the
friendship, per se; I was just made aware of her boundaries and
then I knew what I could ask of her and what she would define as
reasonable. This was a very important lesson to me as I found that
not everyone's definition of friendship is the same.

In her book, *The Friendships of Women*, Dee Brestin talks
about learning to discern an "alligator friend" from a "rose friend."
Alligators are the type of friends who are "all teeth." They attack,
they are predators, and they do not have your best interests at

heart. "Rose" friends are the women who have a few thorns, but the beauty and aroma they add to your life are worth the risk of occasionally getting your finger pricked. You know the thorns are there, but they're minor in comparison to the joy that the rose brings. It is sometimes a long journey to knowing what type of friend you're dealing with.

Intimacy with a true friend requires a higher level of commitment from those of us who are followers of Jesus. Because there is a spiritual element that permeates our friendship, we take on spiritual responsibilities: honesty, accountability, and a commitment to pray for her. There is something about praying for a friend that draws you closer, and the intimate knowledge you have of her life allows you to pray in a way that other people cannot. It is so comforting to know that a friend who is walking the same spiritual journey as you can "have your back" in prayer for your life and your needs. It is also a privilege to provide spiritual intercession on behalf of your friend.

In the classic story *Anne of Green Gables*, Anne Shirley was overjoyed when she found her "bosom friend," Diana Barry. The girls came from very different backgrounds and social stations, but they shared confidences, were there for each other in crises, and grew up into adulthood together. Anne even held back Diana's hair as she lost her lunch after imbibing a little too much raspberry cordial. Now that's a real litmus test of friendship! And you just can't do that sort of thing on MySpace.

We all need friends, because if we didn't have them, with whom could we discuss our families?

Ah, families. Another area we need to decorate, because our family is what it is. No one can go back in time and magically change their family of origin. You can change your name at the courthouse, but the DNA from which you sprang will have its way. You may believe your parents came from Area 54 and that you *had* to be adopted because you don't fit in with these people. Maybe you *were* adopted and you always hoped that your biological parents (surely superior beings from another planet) would one day return to pick you up and take you to your real home far, far away. But your childhood is done, it was what it was, and your family is your family. You cannot change your birth order, whether or not both your parents stayed or left the family, or the ability of your parents to understand or adequately parent you. As surely as you were called to be where you are today in your life, your family of origin—the good, the bad, the ugly—was part of the formation of who you are today. For those who had horrible experiences in their childhoods, this may be hard to believe. Sometimes adults do things to children that are outright evil. Sometimes they are malicious. Relatives whose intentions are good can still accidentally hurt us deeply. Even if you had a great family, there were times in your growing up years that you didn't feel like you were accepted or supported. This may have caused an emotional wound that is still part of you today.

I am not a huge fan of *The Godfather* Trilogy. I can't understand what they're saying half the time, and I can't figure out who started what with whom and why it has to end with so much blood, but I do know that *la famiglia* is *muy importante* (I know,

I'm mixing my languages, but you get my drift). Loyalty matters. Family matters. That I understand. I'm somewhat envious of medieval times (not the plagues and the beheadings, though) because families had crests. These were pictorial representations of the values a family stood for. I once tried to figure out what would be the four symbols on our crest . . . hmmm. I would have to say they would be a Bible (for obvious reasons), a crossed knife and fork (we love to eat), a comedy mask (we love to laugh), and the ESPN logo. In all seriousness, I think our motto across the top would be *Familia suppetiae* (Latin for "family shows up," which is quite ironic considering we're out of town most of the time). But we have made efforts to be present for important moments in each other's lives. We did almost miss Austin's preparation for his high school homecoming dance date. We were driving in from an out-of-state event and we wheeled in five minutes before he was about to leave, just in time to help him tie his bow tie and snap a couple of photos before he peeled out of the driveway. (I didn't say family shows up *early*, we just show up.) And the first time I performed at a large arena event my whole family showed up to support me. As cool as all the noise of the applause was from the attendees, it was simply priceless to have the people with me who had experienced the whole ride.

Familia suppetiae also means that we show up in the hard times, in the moments of intense disappointment and sorrow, in the times when no one else would understand. Family = We. It's the Renfroe "crest." And sometimes that gets us in situations that "we" would rather not be involved in. It's like when the Lone

Ranger and Tonto were riding along through the sagebrush and suddenly about a million Indians came riding over the hill. The two heroes were surrounded, and things were looking pretty bad for them. The Lone Ranger turned to Tonto and said, "Tonto, we're surrounded. What are we going to do?" Tonto turned to the Lone Ranger and replied, "What you mean 'we,' white man?" The joke is funny, but "we" is the defining feature of family (at least it's supposed to be). Family walks in when the rest of the world walks out. I pray that our family can honor this value as long as we're on this earth.

We have an extended family member who is a young man making his way toward independence in his life. Whenever we visit in his home we are amazed that he talks about his mother and their personal family issues in front of us and her. He will bring up his mother's perceived failures and enumerate the ways in which her parenting when he was nine years old is the root of all his current problems. I think it may be his way of saying things to his mother that he would never say to her one-on-one, but, wow, is it ever uncomfortable for us to listen to. To her credit, she doesn't "get back at him" — at least not in front of us. To his credit, I am not his mother because that boy might be short a few of his teeth if he chose to air his resentments for General Public Consumption. What's ironic is that we do not think less of his mom, we think less of him for his apparent inability to discern what is appropriate discussion material and to move past his past. At a certain point we all have to accept responsibility for how we're going to proceed with life regardless of all the things that happen in our family of origin, and we have the ability to choose whether we are going to rehearse our familial injustices until the cows come home or put them in a better frame and move on.

So how do we decorate these people closest to us, the family members who have had such a major role in our formative years and the friends who open us up for a lifetime of risk and benefit? Daniel Goleman, PhD, author of *Emotional Intelligence*, said in an interview with *O Magazine*, "Relationships . . . help you repair bad things that happened to you in the past. The most potent shaping of the brain occurs in our key early relationships. But it goes on all our lives, and nurturing relationships later in life can rewrite the neural scripts from childhood."

In our lives, family shapes the beginning, friends (according to the above quote) can help us reshape how we *view* our beginnings. I pray that we can find new frames in our hearts to treasure them all.

if you're happy and you know it, you're probably annoying someone who isn't

When I was growing up on a farm in Texas, I remember my grandmother telling me that I might need to play a little more gently with a puppy. "Be careful," she cautioned. "You might make him mean." I couldn't understand it but I figured Nana knew what she was talking about. I remember wondering how that worked. Could you really change a nice dog into a mean dog just by playing rough with him? If that was the case, it might explain a lot about crabby people, including my elementary school librarian. (Please, no hate mail from the Really Nice Librarian's Society. I know you must exist, just not in my childhood.)

Psychologists have gone around and around this subject for years, whether "nature" (your DNA and emotional hardwiring that you come with at birth) is the biggest factor in a person's temperament, or if "nurture" (your upbringing, surroundings, and experiences) is more important to your formation. If professionals have been arguing about a subject matter for years, I generally find it best to stay out from in between them. But as a card-carrying member of the human race and a mom, I know what I know about myself and my family. I know that there are things in my basic temperament that cannot be accounted for in my upbringing or experiences, and there are things that may have come with my original emotional hardwiring that have been practically eradicated because of my life experiences. So at the risk of practicing psychology without a license, I am going to go out on a limb here and say, "It's both."

If you have had more than one child, then you already know that kids come with their own little personalities firmly intact upon arrival. Each one has strong opinions about The Way the World Ought to Be, and we are somehow supposed to decode this through their various cries and coos and sleeping patterns and what shows up in their diapers—somewhat like reading tea leaves. It requires a great deal of trial and error and some maternal intuition, but after a while you crack the Unique Newborn Code for this individual. You can try the same approach you tried with another child, but this one will let you know that prior approaches are not gonna fly here. It can drive us mothers to distraction but affirms our suspicions about the role of each child's individual bent and how well-formed it is by the time our little ones are ejected from our wombs.

I remember being a young mother and trying to figure out how my three children could have all taken up prenatal residence in the same womb-space yet be so incredibly different. Didn't John and I donate the same DNA every time? Did I not carry them in the same belly? Was it the Fudgesicles and butter beans I ate? What could account for this individuality?

It was during my children's preschool years that I first heard Florence Littauer on a radio show. On that program she was discussing the four basic personality types and how your temperament bent would cause you to respond in certain ways to life. It was fascinating to listen to her categorizations and think of my own temperament and that of the people closest to me. She talked about the Choleric type (those who are strong and bossy, sometimes stubborn), the Melancholy type (assessors, analyzers, with a tendency toward "overanalysis paralysis"), the Sanguines ("party on," friendly, social types with a tendency toward unreliability), and the Phlegmatics (indifferent, indecisive, relaxed). As Florence put it, "A Choleric likes it 'my way,' a Melancholy likes it 'the right way,' a Sanguine likes it 'the fun way,' and a Phlegmatic likes it 'any way.'" I wanted to order the cassette copy of the program, but not being a Melancholy I had no idea where I could find a pencil. What's sad is that we don't really have any true Melancholics in our family, so none of us knows where the pencils are.

Then Gary Smalley and John Trent gave the same types different names in their attempt to make "personality typing" accessible and easily understood for families. They used animals—lions, beavers, otters, and golden retrievers—to make personality types simple and fun to remember. Sort of an Animal Planet approach. All these were loosely based upon the D.I.S.C. personality analysis system—Dominant (decisive doers), Influential (inspiring interactors), Steady (stable supporters), and Conscientious (cautious correctors). If you've never had any sort of temperament analysis you can probably identify yourself even from this short explanation, but I would encourage you to find out more about the way you and the other members of your family (as well as your friends) are hardwired. It is a great tool in gaining understanding of another person's point of view. That is, if you are interested in their viewpoint.

I find that when I'm in the middle of a discussion I am usually trying to persuade everyone that *my* perspective is the correct one; I am not necessarily interested in understanding *theirs*. (Hint: This would make me the Choleric/Lion/Dominant "my way or the highway" type.) I have a couple of signs in my office (okay, so I have a *lot* of signs in my office. I love words and love to have words around me) that say things like, "Get over it, get on with it" and "Put on your big girl panties and deal with it." Not too compassionate, eh? They represent one approach to reality: just stiffening the upper lip and moving forward without looking back. Sometimes that is a great idea. Sometimes it's the worst thing you could do. My take-charge personality has some advantages, but I can occasionally leave people with my tire marks across them when I exit the room. Not pretty.

Personality typing, while potentially enlightening and helpful, can be taken to its extreme. If we use it to box or label ourselves or others, we can discount our individuality and ignore the subtle nuances that make us the complex creatures God designed. Take, for instance, the fact that I'm a Dominant type, but I just can *not* jump into a swimming pool. This is somewhat embarrassing when the rest of my family just dives right in with no heed of the water temperature. They don't even stick a toe in to get a hint before they jump. It's insanity, I tell you. I'm a *slow pool enterer*. Painfully slow. I don't know why I torture myself like this. John is always saying, "It's easier if you just jump in." I am intellectually aware of this. This is not news to me. But as I am inching myself into the water I always stop short of The Girls. The cold pool water is such a shock to them. They want to remain warm. They do not want to become cold and wet. Plus, I have a big nose. I don't like the chlorine up my nose and it doesn't look cool to jump in while holding your nose. Finally, the negative anticipation becomes overwhelming, and I have to take the rest of the plunge (if you could term resentfully dipping the bust to neck area "plunging"). But the buildup to this normally lasts about ten minutes. Ten minutes of my life doing what could have been done in two seconds if I had just jumped in. Very un-take-charge behavior from a certified lion.

In the workplace or a committee setting the mix of different temperaments will more often than not lead to a reasonable plan of action, with the Dominants casting the vision and leading the charge, the Influencers believing that all things are possible, the Conscientious making lists of how we get from point A to point B as well as every potential pitfall, and the Steady ones just happy that a decision was arrived at and everyone is still on board.

In the marriage arena, the animals invariably mix it up according to the cliché "opposites attract." Then, once the marriage is underway, opposites *attack*. The tendencies that seemed so charming about the person because they are different and create a balance in our universe become the very traits that cause us to bang our heads against hard objects. Thank God that He sent John into my life, as he is so steady and people-oriented that he helps to temper my tendency to charge ahead without taking another's feelings into account. And my strong sense that things will work out (Dominants believe they can power their way through anything; you know, we're the people who write the songs like "Ain't No Mountain High Enough") serves to jump-start his pragmatic, analytical side. I believe that God's divine design brings us to these unions in order that we may have a daily opportunity to demonstrate our faith by choosing not to kill our spouse, and also to give us the emotional "sandpaper" we need to take off some of our personality-type edges. Oh, and to provide endless material for comedians. I'm particularly grateful for that.

Regardless of our temperament, we are all seeking to understand others and how to better get along. Developing an empathetic imagination may be the result of mellowing that comes with age and experience, but it helps to think of a scenario some experts use to show how a rush to judgment can be flawed. Imagine yourself at a red light. You are on your way to an important meeting and you are late, so you are agitated when the car in front of you does not move when the light turns green. You start fuming at how idiotic the driver of that car is for not paying attention and noticing that the light is green. "This always happens to me," you say out loud to no one but yourself. Your blood pressure is rising, you are just about to lay on your horn to let him know how lame he is when he gets out of the car. Well! Things are going from bad to worse because now he is definitely *not* going to move, and you are going to miss the light and, in your mind, the world might just come to an end. Then you notice that he goes around to the passenger side and lifts a frail elderly woman out onto the sidewalk and starts administering CPR. What happens to your feelings of anger and resentment? Do you imagine that they would be completely gone in that instant of realization of what was really going on? You would quickly move from anger to empathy to a desire to help all in a moment, and your "emergency" would suddenly seem less urgent in light of a life in the balance.

This may be hard to replicate when someone in the workplace is not moving as fast as you would like on a project or a member of your family is not understanding you for the hundredth time, but many times there are reasons for their behavior, not always as evident as a case of cardiac arrest, but just as real. When we seek to understand instead of assuming the worst, we operate from a whole different vantage point. When Jesus Himself says to us, "Don't judge because it will happen to you," He is underscoring our entirely human tendency to believe that the way we view the world is the way everyone (who has a lick of sense) *should* view the world. C. S. Lewis said that if we held everyone else to the same standard we hold ourselves to, we would have absolutely no problem getting along with anyone, as our ability to justify our actions knows no bounds.

We all have a default emotional state and basic set of tendencies that, when left to our own evaluation, make perfect sense to us. It's a part of the remarkable diversity in human interactions and the reason many of us feel like pulling out our hair on a regular basis. Wouldn't it be great if we all wore T-shirts every day that had our own personal set of incredibly well-developed preferences printed on them so that we could know exactly what to expect from each other? That would be so convenient. Then at least we'd know exactly what we were doing that was giving the other person hives.

In our house we call it "Rules," and brother, does everyone in our household have their own special set. You can identify yours by filling in "Never/Always" statements ("I never _____." "I always _____."). And all of you people reading this who are in denial about the fact that you *have* them, that's your personal Rule #1: "I never have any rules."

I will start with myself (just to be fair). I have a Rule about the tops of things. I like them. Just the tops. Not the bottoms. I like just the tops of muffins. Not the part that would be contained in the muffin cup, but the top part that's just a little bigger than the cup. I also like the top bite of a banana. I like to lie with one leg on top of the covers, and I dig the foam on top of a cappuccino. I always take more clothes than I need to take on a trip (I like options), and I never file papers immediately. I feel they need to sit out in the open air for a while before they are crushed in the cruel file folders forever.

John's list consists of: Never should any items of mine be on his side of the bed, and no one can enter his closet without him hyperventilating. He must have cornbread with greens, and he cannot bring himself to discard a *Sports Illustrated* magazine until it has been in the bathroom three weeks. My mom's Rules are that no one may come to the kitchen in the morning without bringing their dirty clothes with them (because we all know that dirty clothes mate if left unsupervised and produce *more* dirty clothes). She also has a Rule that all dishes must be heated before the hot food or beverages can be served in them. I am not sure if she was very cold for long periods of time as a child or what, but the coffee cups and carafe have to be heated up (with hot water from the microwave) before the coffee can be brewed, and the plates for dinner have to be heated up so that the food won't cool off too soon. Never mind that we are all burning our fingers on the hot edges. She would have them sizzling like the fajita plates at the Mexican restaurant if she had her way. She also has no respect for John's closet rule and goes in there when we are out of town to hang up his freshly laundered shirts.

Our kids have their Rules, too. Calvin has one about replacing his expended calories immediately after a workout. We have actually been twenty minutes away from serving a big dinner and Calvin will be over in the corner of the kitchen with the blender whipping up his power shake because he just came back from lifting weights. I'll look at him and say, "But we're eating in twenty minutes," and he'll say, "Mom, you know I have to do this. I just worked out." It's a Rule. Calvin also must be with people all the time. If he is awake there must be a friend or cohort within range. This is only temporarily interrupted by school or work activities, and even there he will make friends so that he can continue to enforce this Rule. Also, if you happen to stand between him and the TV when the ESPN channel is on, he gets highly agitated.

Austin's first Rule is that he never wants to stop whatever he is doing at the time. I have no idea why this is, but whatever he is doing at the moment is the most important thing he has ever done, and he perceives any interruption in the doing of that thing as a direct threat. It doesn't matter if the thing you are asking that he start doing is his favorite thing in the world, he doesn't want to stop doing the current thing to do the alternate thing. It's like he has no personal "clutch" to shift from one activity to the next, and you can almost hear the mental gears "grinding" while he struggles through the transition. At that point, whatever the new activity is *becomes* the one he is now committed to and doesn't want to stop. Austin also has a Rule about Most Favored Outfit Status. If a particular outfit is one that he is enamored with, he is capable of wearing it over and over again. And again. Come to think of it, I guess that's just an extension of his Rule #1.

Now we come to Baby Girl Elyse, the Rule Ruler. She has a Rule for just about every letter of the alphabet. Her sheets and covers can't ever touch the floor (there are bugs down there). She will only drink out of glasses with pleasing shapes. She never sets her purse on the floorboards of cars. She always gets upset if someone touches her hair, and she never likes to pack her shoes in the same suitcase as her clothes. One Rule she and I share in common is the reading of the virgin magazines. (This is when a magazine is freshest and the best information is available only for the first person who reads it. If it's already been read by someone else it loses its thrill.)

I guess we all have our lists of "always" and "nevers." Maybe the trick is in not letting The Rules rule us to the point of insanity. After all, any of our Rules are really just preferences taken to the extreme. But it does help to realize what these are in our lives and to try to accommodate those of the people we love. Besides that, knowing each others' Rules gives us great ammunition to pick on each other!

I also believe (along with many other people smarter than myself, therefore it must be true) that we all come with a "happiness quotient," if you will, a basic propensity to feel hopeful and positive about life in general. The Glass Half Empties ("The sun will not rise tomorrow") will probably never understand the Glass Half Fulls ("The sun will never stop shining!"). Abraham Lincoln once said that most folks are about as happy as they make up their minds to be. I find this interesting coming from a man who struggled with bouts of severe depression for most of his life and was married to a woman with manic-depressive tendencies. President Lincoln had embraced this truth: You may have a default emotional state, but you have the power to choose if you allow it to control you. With his default state leaning hard toward melancholy, he refused to dwell in his negative thoughts or to allow those thoughts to deter him from his purpose of leading the Union in the darkest days of our nation's history.

We are also affected by something that psychologists call the "resiliency factor." This would be the measure of our emotional "rubber content" — meaning how quickly we can bounce back from setbacks and adversity. We all know a few people who seem to be practically made of this emotional rubber and can "boing-oing-oing-oing" right back up on their feet almost immediately. I don't know if these people have stronger faith or maybe just a little less general awareness, but whatever the reason, hardships have a hard time keeping them down for long. They are like those little toys that were famous for their ability to pop back up: "Weebles wobble but they don't fall down." And then there are the others—the ones who have a great deal less resiliency in their nature. For these people it is a particular struggle to recover from any sort of setback. They need time and space to begin to see the light of day again. This is an important factor to consider when trying to decide how to help someone through a rough time. If they don't have much emotional rubber, they are gonna need a little more time than the average bear.

In his book, *Happiness: What Studies on Twins Show Us about Nature, Nurture, and the Happiness Set Point*, University of Minnesota professor emeritus of psychology David Lykken maintains that all of us have a genetic set point for happiness (just as we have for eye color, hair color, build, etc.), but we are not helpless in the hands of our "genetic steersman." Lykken writes, "Happiness is genetically influenced, although it is not genetically fixed. The brain's structure can be modified through practice. If you really want to be happier than your grandparents provided for in your genes, you have to learn the kinds of things you can do, day by day, to bounce your set point up and avoid the things that bounce it down." His book details studies of identical twins raised in different environments and argues that an individual's set point determines about 50 percent of their disposition to happiness. In other words, some people are *happy*, regardless of their less-than-ideal circumstances, while others are *unhappy*, even when they seem to "have it all."

We could all take a quick glance around our circle of acquaintances and see that happiness is not tied to acquisitions or accomplishments; it is a combination of our set point and our choices. "Materialism is toxic for happiness," says University of Illinois psychologist Ed Diener. "Even rich materialists aren't as happy as those who care less about getting and spending." And our level of physical health, once touted as the key to happiness ("If you've got your health, you've got it all!"), only seems to be a factor if a person is critically ill. Objective health measures don't relate to life satisfaction, but how you *feel* about your physical well-being does. We could all name some perfectly healthy people who take their health for granted and are not any happier because of it, while some chronically ill folks often bear up well, and hypochondriacs make themselves and everyone around them miserable despite the fact that there's nothing physically wrong with them.

Recent studies in neurology and chemistry (don't you just love those little pictures where they show you actual brain activity and how it lights up in different areas in response to stimuli? It's like God made the original video game in our heads!) have given us the ability to see that as we choose our thoughts we can actually change our brain activity. This is pretty remarkable when you consider that we are who God made us to be, yet we still get to choose every day who we are becoming. Other studies on brain imaging are backing up what Scripture has told us for centuries. Richard Davidson, professor of psychology at the University of Wisconsin, found in his research that high levels of activity at the left frontal area of the cerebral cortex coincided with feelings of happiness, joy, and alertness. Activity on the right frontal area corresponded to feelings of sadness, anxiety, and worry. Since meditation generates more left-brain activity, studies have concluded that meditation and prayer produce a happier person. Well, looky there! God was right again! Imagine that.

If you are the way you are, and other people are the way they are, where does that leave us? In a continual state of frustration because our temperaments are so different? When we come to any kind of a standoff, does our unspoken dialogue run something like this?

I don't understand you at all. I don't know why you do what you do and why you can't just do things the way I want them done. Is this really so hard? If you really

a. loved me
b. cared about me
c. understood me

everything would be so easy. What is wrong with *you*?!

Be honest. Don't we spend a lot of time wishing the people around us would Get with the Program? Namely, My Program?

What a colossal waste of time and energy. They can't get on My Program because they are really busy wishing I would get with Their Program. We have so many tools at our disposal to learn about our friends and family, to gain insight on what makes them tick and how the world looks through their grid. Recognizing that you have a Default Emotional State (and so does everyone you come in contact with) is the first step to decorating (appreciating) it so that you will not, in fact, drive everyone around you absolutely insane.

if love is blind, that explains a lot

I've never been a bridesmaid. I'm trying to figure out what this says about me. Could it mean:

A. I wasn't forming meaningful attachments to other marriageable age females when I was in the eighteen to twenty-nine age range? Or
B. All my friends knew that I wouldn't be able to refrain from laughing uncontrollably during the ceremony and didn't want to risk it? Or
C. I gave off the "I will not buy an ugly dress no matter how much I think of you personally" vibe? Or
D. I was always the pianist or soloist.

I think it was probably D (it's easier to find friends who will buy the ugly dress than one who kept up with the piano lessons). Since I could play something more elaborate than "Heart and Soul" or "Chopsticks," I was once the bride, always the wedding musician, and never once the bridesmaid. I have considered working up to a full-blown state of feeling that I might have missed out on a wonderful slice of life, but when I take the time to enumerate the duties of each I find it hard to complain.

Bridesmaid _____

Buy the (usually) ugly dress and all necessary accessories

Attend several showers with gifts for each shower in support for your friend, the bride

Sit through four-hour rehearsal so you are sure where to stand and how fast to process and whose arm you take to recess

Get hair done to match hair of other bridesmaids so that there will be total fashion uniformity

Arrive at wedding early for makeup and photos in 100 degree weather

Stand at the ceremony for an hour in shoes that really hurt (but they're custom-dyed to match the dress so you definitely cannot wear them with anything else)

Stand longer at the reception, by now the feet have swollen and the straps of the shoes are cutting off various toes

Remember to take the dress to a Goodwill store in another town on Monday

Pianist _____

Provide lovely accompaniment for most important day of bride's life, sometimes even get paid for it!

So, all in all, pianist trumps bridesmaid.

I had two bridesmaids in my wedding and, as much as I loved my friends, their big contribution (besides wearing bad lavender dresses that made me seem outstanding—the true calling of the bridesmaid) was going out to purchase not one but *two* Hershey's chocolate bars to fend off the sudden onset of heretofore unheard of levels of stress. (In the FYI department, a chocolate bar should be standard issue with the sewing kit, scotch tape, oscillating fan, and the single-use emergency Valium pill that comes with the bride's dressing room.)

As little girls we get the Complete Dream Package reiterated to us over and over and over again. In the fairy tales, in the movies made out of the fairy tales, in the lunchboxes from the movies from the fairy tales, the message is the same: A whirlwind romance will result in an effortless wedding immediately followed by "happily ever after." The pinnacle, the peak, the penultimate. Beautiful girl + handsome guy = happily ever after. If this were true, all the beautiful stars who marry other beautiful stars should have the formula down.

The phrase "and they lived happily ever after" had to be created by the writers of children's stories who didn't (a) have any more ideas of how to continue the story, or (b) didn't want to scare the little children with the truth. What they might have more accurately written was, "and they lived together, learned how to tolerate each other's idiosyncrasies, overcame urges to do physical harm, and built a life history together, complete with intermittent periods of deep affection, interrupted by insane busy-ness and wild emotional swings between hope and disappointment (hoping for the best, forgiving the worst)." And even if you find your "soul mate" you will find that his "soul" will gladly let you fall into the toilet at 2 a.m. if you don't teach him Proper Seat Etiquette. I am fairly sure I never heard *that* in any of the fairy tales I was told.

I don't know about the "soul mate" idea, as it intimates that there is a perfect person for you, one who completes you and has the elusive "it," and you'll just know it when you find it. There might be an internal "ping" that lets you know this person has a special attraction for you, but perhaps the "soul mate" idea is just too much pressure. And if it is true in the divine sense, it means that the enemy of our soul (Satan) is probably trying his best to keep this union from occurring. Wouldn't that be great to trot out during your next argument? "That's right, honey. You were just a tool of the Devil to keep me from finding my true soul mate!" (I don't recommend it.) It is a wonderful thing when two hearts with common values choose to commit themselves to each other and create a family together, but in all my years of living and observing couples I can truly say that even the "happiest ever after" had its share of bumps and potholes.

Here is a rarely admitted truth: No matter how fulfilling the marriage, there are women who are married who spend part of their days dreaming about being single. And no matter how full their life is otherwise, there are single women who spend a good part of their time wishing they were married.

I do know that the Bible emphasizes the many benefits of remaining single. It's not super-comforting when you're the single

person, but the married chicks could point out a few benefits for
you:

No one judging your housekeeping skills.

Nobody to point out that a second Kate Spade bag may be
frivolous.

The toilet seat—permanently down.

You can live your own brand of romance.

That's right. I said "romance." I think it's a misconception
that you can live a romantic life only if you're in love (and living
happily ever after). In my humble opinion, some of the most
romantic people I know are not married or even dating. These
single women refuse to let that detail diminish their capacity for
romance—richness of experience, enjoyment, love, and fulfill-
ment. They have a sense of abundance and an appreciation for
lovely experiences. They are true romantics, without men. Now,
I also know that many of them would trade it in for some hot
monogamy should God so lead, but they aren't letting their life
slip by uncelebrated.

And if you are one of my single sisters, may I just encourage
you with a story that my mother-in-law related to me? Vesta told
me that she was going about her grocery shopping one day when
she witnessed a man poking his finger through a plastic wrap-
per, into the cookie package, to "test" the freshness of the cookies. Then he put the opened package back and got an unopened
one to purchase. What a great illustration of guys in general:
They may want to test the "cookies," but they want to marry the
"unopened package." Don't compromise your purity or integrity

for somebody who's just poking around. *Capiche?*

Whether you aren't (and wish you were) or are (and sometimes wish you weren't) married—or you've decided that the person you're married to R-E-A-L-L-Y needs to be someone else—it is what it is. Learning to love the one you're with (maybe it's you!) is a tall order, but not impossible with some "interior" decoration. Maybe love *is* blind (and if you're single that may be why it can't find you!). If you're married it may be a good trait to pull out every now and then in order to mercifully overlook a few faults and decide if every issue is really worth all the drama.

There are all sorts of ways to foster a happy union. I read about a couple who had been married for forty-five years and had raised a brood of eleven children and were blessed with twenty-two grandchildren. When asked the secret for staying together all that time, the wife replied, "Many years ago we made a promise that the first one to pack up and leave had to take all the kids." I guess that would be considered their "pre-nup." John and I didn't have one, basically because we came to the marriage with nothin'. Ours would have had to read, "Should this union dissolve, I'll take my debts, you take yours." Don't laugh. Some days it was the only thought that kept us hanging on.

It's not surprising that we would have a hard time finding Happily Ever After when our brains are somewhat predisposed to make it harder. We comedians have been joking about this for years, but there is now scientific evidence to back it up. I submit for your consideration the latest findings in a book by neurologist Louann Brizendine called (okay, so the title isn't too creative—maybe she's another Mensa) *The Female Brain.* In her years of clinical research the good doctor has deduced that 99 percent of the genetics between men and women are the same . . . but what a difference that 1 percent makes!

For example:

- Male brains are larger by 9 percent, but women have the same number of brain cells densely packed into a smaller skull (obviously our cells are more petite).
- Connecting through talking activates the pleasure centers in a girl's brain, causing a major dopamine and oxytocin rush. In other words, we feel happy when we're connected. (This is news?)
- Early on, female ovaries begin producing huge amounts of estrogen that marinate the girl's brain and spur the growth of brain circuits and centers for connection. (This explains it: We can't help our need for connection, we were marinated for it.)
- Men have two and a half times the brain space devoted to sexual drive as women do, as well as larger brain centers for action and aggression. (Fill in your own comment here: _____.)
- The areas of the brain that track emotion and memory formation are larger and more sensitive in the female brain. (This explains a lot.)
- Men notice subtle signs of sadness in a face only 40 percent of the time, while women pick up on them 90 percent of

the time. (This is why your account of fifteen minutes at any social gathering will vary *wildly* from his—he was missing 60 percent of the action!)

We not only vary in brain wiring, but our approach to almost any endeavor will point out our gender differences. Take, for instance, the fact that John has "a thing" for the little automated voice that is in our car's GPS system. I have been trying to figure out why he is so attracted to her, but one day he broke it down for me like this:

Anita says:	GPS girl says:
Where are we going? Why are you making me decide again? I hate it when you make me be the one to choose. You choose this time. I'm not going to decide.	
	Enter destination.
You can't go that way, the road is too wind-y, it makes me nauseous. Why can't you take the direct route like everybody else?	
	Calculating route.
You're in the wrong lane, you're gonna miss the exit. I don't know why you stay in the left lane so long. You're gonna miss it, I said!	
	Prepare to exit.
Great. You missed it. I told you that you were going to miss it. You always miss it. Now we're never gonna get off this highway.	
	Recalculating route.

I ask you, what wife could compete with Little Miss Techno-Calm??

I happen to be married to a very patient and loving man. I have discussed in previous books the gazillion ways he proves his love all the time, so I will not bore you with reiterating his many sterling qualities. But even Mr. Sterling can get on a girl's last nerve, you know what I'm saying? He doesn't understand my "pile" system of organization and tidies them up (or as I call it, "loses my stuff"). He has intermittent recurring deafness (selective hearing). He drives like we're on the Indy 500 racetrack and has never met a parking space that he liked (consequently we will "try out" several before he settles on yet another inferior one). As my friend Thelma Wells says, "Honey, there's somethin' wrong with everything!"

For example, I have a love/hate relationship with my cell phone. This has been going on for a solid ten plus years. I am conflicted because I alternately wonder how we ever functioned without them and exactly how I might smash mine to cause it the most horrible death. This is largely due to the phenomenon known as "the drop-out zone." This is that moment when you are deep into the story about how there was just one pair left in your size on the 75 percent off rack and you suddenly realize that where you have left a space for your best friend to "ooh" and "ah" concerning your shopping superiority, there is now only this strange digital silence. Your call has been unceremoniously "dropped." You are disconnected and your antennae bars are nil. This is the moment that makes those commercials where the guy is testing the cell phone coverage by continually saying, "Can you hear me now?" seem like reality TV.

That's assuming you can even *find* your cell phone when it rings, since cell phones are now smaller than credit cards. Back in the eighties if you were in possession of a "mobile" phone, it was bolted to your car. Then a few years later we got the "bag phone," which you could tote with you, but it was hardly worth it. Plus the airtime was exorbitant back then—about $5 per minute. Now we have the luxury of 3,000 minutes a month so we can yak and yak and yak about anything and everything or *nothing* at all. This has bred a new level of laziness in our household. My children will pick up their cell phones and call from the basement up to the house line to ask if dinner will be ready soon. I would call John's cell to tell him when it's time to come in from the yard for dinner, but he can't hear it unless I'm standing next to him to tell him that it's ringing. Sorta defeats the purpose, huh?

I distinctly recall when I was engaged to marry John I thought to myself, *Oh, how glorious it will be to marry this man who will want to hear every precious syllable that will ever pass across my lips! And I can't wait to delve into his emotional state on a daily basis, during which time we will reach new heights of passionate verbal bliss! We will live in Communication Nirvana!* Turns out that marriage is full of Unintentional Dropout Zones. You think you are imparting information and feelings, you feel you are making some progress toward mutual understanding, and suddenly you notice that his eyes have glazed over and you realize that he definitely cannot "hear you now." And it's not always because of disinterest or indifference; sometimes it is rooted in the very things that bring you great comfort—history and familiarity.

These lead us to assumptions that we know how our spouse has thought and acted in the past, therefore we don't really need to have that conversation all over again. We can believe that we have them all figured out and become emotionally lazy, drifting apart without realizing it.

Those of us who are married probably came with our own set of illusions regarding how perfect and wonderful everything would be. As the days unfolded we may have been jolted into the realization that things weren't exactly as we imagined they would be. We became aware that there is, indeed, something wrong with everything—and everyone. It's important to remember that, should you have the grace to hold on and press through in the commitment of marriage, there will come a time when the illusions that were so deeply held in the beginning will be one by one replaced by a lifetime of things that are real: sacrifice, trust, faith in each other, and a love that has stood the tests of time.

I remember a couple of years ago John asked me what I wanted for Christmas. Without hesitation I responded, "Eye contact." He smiled as if to say, "Good one. Now tell me what you *really* want so that I can wrap it up and put it under the tree." But that really *was* what I wanted. More eye contact. Guess what? I got it. Sometimes we have to be clear about what it is we need and not be afraid to ask for it.

In the New Testament we read this sage advice: "My dear brothers, take note of this: Everyone should be quick to listen, slow to speak and slow to become angry" (James 1:19). It's an interesting order, don't you think? I have to stop speaking in order to listen (seems logical, but for the highly verbal it's easier *said* than done). Then I have to engage with my ears, my eyes, and my heart. Then I have to choose to move my normal knee-jerk reaction of anger to the bottom of the list. Wow, tough assignment! But this constitutes the Love Sandwich—shutting up being the top layer of bread, resisting anger being the bottom piece of bread, and *really listening* being the main ingredient.

In our marriage of nearly twenty-five years, John and I are learning to work hard at enhancing our Personal Wireless Network to the point that we can eradicate the Unintentional Dropout Zone and be the #1 service provider for each other. We don't want to miss a thing.

So, for us, the question could read like this:

Can (Could it continue to be possible . . .)

You (that the person to whom I've entrusted my heart for life . . .)

Hear (truly understand, engaging fully with me on a head and heart level . . .)

Me (knowing it all—the good, the bad, the ugly, the quirky . . .)

Now (not based on last week's, last month's, last year's info, but what I'm thinking now)?

If we listen with our ears, our eyes, and our heart, may our answer to the one we love forever be, "Loud and clear, baby. Loud and clear."

Chapter 8

if you can conceive it, you can support it for the rest of its life

A few years back Dr. Kevin Lehman wrote a book that captured the essence of most every parent's challenge: *Making Your Children Mind Without Losing Yours*. Which sheds further light on that old saying, "Insanity is hereditary—you get it from your kids."

When your kids are small, people will say to you, "Treasure every moment. They grow up so fast. Don't blink or you'll miss it." I think I speak for a host of women when I say, we blinked. A lot. Blinking, blinking, blinking—hoping to skip over just a *little* bit of it. As a former mother to multiple simultaneous preschoolers let me say that some days are just like the movie *Groundhog Day* where Bill Murray gets to live the same day over and over and over and over again. It feels like that—the same Cheerios, the same apple juice, the same questions, the same laundry. I'm not saying that it's not wonderful, just r-e-a-l-l-y familiar (blink, blink).

When you find yourself under the dining room table with a blanket pulled over your head for the seventeenth game of hide and seek *today*, don't you sometimes wonder, "Who are these little people, and why do they think I'm responsible for them?" Then one of them finds you and gives you a grape-jelly kiss and you remember, "Oh, these *are* my kids." And the thoughts of loving and cherishing them are intermixed with thoughts of, "Am I damaging them? Am I doing this thing right?" We are given a great deal of responsibility in the development of our kids, but sometimes it can cross over from "good parenting" into "my project." And like it or not, kids will keep it real.

It's a good thing that I have thick skin, because the dinner table discussion at my house when all the kids are home will often devolve into a "Let's Recall the Most Random Things Mom Did to Us" throwdown. (I allow this to go on *only* because they are: (a) all still alive to tell the tale, so none of it was fatal, and (b) it's pretty funny stuff.) They accuse me of such ridiculous things as adjusting the "latest research" facts to support whatever item we happened to have on hand. (Upset stomach? Let me see . . . "We have ginger ale. Yes, ginger ale is the best for upset stomach. What? I did *not* say 7-Up the last time!" Nosebleed? Hmm, no ice . . . "I read the other day that a wet towel will stop that bleeding.") So maybe I had a couple of Creative Research Statistics—I needed backup. My offspring weren't going to take my word for it.

They will also accuse me of making up fantasy games to cover up my failure to get to the grocery store. If I forgot to pick up milk for their cereal the night before, I would tell them to pretend that they had crash landed in the African Congo and had to make do with their military rations. My boys would remind me that MREs come with powdered milk and water, so I was not even upholding the Geneva Convention's minimum requirements for the treatment of POWs. Why did I ever let them watch The History Channel?

We may have more of a handle on emotionally "decorating" our kids because we have spent years decorating them otherwise. We dress them up for pictures, decorate their rooms, decorate their birthday cakes and parties, and decorate them for Halloween costumes. I've publicly admitted that I've never seen the value in paying for costumes for Halloween. I never minded my kids going out to score some candy, but not if we had to buy something to wear in order for them to do it. So I would come up with such brilliant Halloween costumes as painting black dots on their faces, cutting out big black spots of construction paper, pinning them to their white sweats, and proclaiming, "Look! You're a dalmatian!" They weren't buying what I was selling, but the need to accrue a plastic pumpkin full of sugared products is a powerful motivator, so they would suck up their pride and trot their spotted selves down the street.

As a minister's wife, may I say that one of the most ill-conceived church activities we ever had was the "Harvest Festival," which was really a sanctified candy-fest. In fact, because church people donated bags of candy to keep the kids "off the street on the Devil's night," our kids got *too much* candy. Our rule was that the plastic pumpkins went up on the top of the refrigerator and they could only choose one tooth-rotting delectable per day. At that rate we

had to throw some out before the Easter Bunny came. That was
how much candy they got at the church Harvest Festival. And
they were told to only come in biblical costumes. Every boy there
was dressed like Moses (no matter what person he was represent-
ing) and every girl looked like Mary, the mother of Jesus. Our
church's version of Halloween resembled a Passion Play being put
on by a midget convention. And our church dentist was passing
out his business cards as the kids bobbed for apples. Good times.

I have always believed in the power of a family mealtime, just
once a day for us to reconnect around food. According to some
psychologists it's one of the leading indicators of how well a child
will do in school. (So if your child is flunking algebra, it might
be your fault.) It's difficult with the types of schedules that most
families keep these days, but I would ask you to really think about
your household and boil it down to the essentials. The question is
whether your kids will recall the third activity you placed them in
this school year or the time you tried to camouflage the butternut
squash under a coating of marshmallows. There are things that
happen around a dining table that just don't happen anywhere
else. It's a time that says, "This is who we are. This is important.
We share life here." That is not to say that it can't be pizza and salad
from a bag, it just has to be regular. Oh, and light a candle. I heard
someone say that it's the only real difference between "eating" and
"dining." Set family meal nights, make them sacrosanct, and don't
let anyone skip. And by all means, let your table be open. If a kid
has a friend over, let them stay for dinner. If they dare.

We could not always enforce the traditional rules of etiquette (like "close your mouth while you are chewing") when multiple children at the table had braces. We have one who can't breathe through his nose half the time, so if he was forced to close his mouth while chewing he would have suffocated. We only had a few hard and fast rules:

1. Napkin in the lap.
2. One bite of a new/offensive food for every year old you are.
3. Bus your own place.

I never understood how hard it could be to get one's plate from point A to point B, but it seemed like we had to remind someone almost every night. Not that we made them *wash* the dishes, or even load the dishwasher—they just had to get their plate and accoutrements from the table to the sink. We didn't think it was too much to ask, but you should have heard the moaning about it. We should have made them load the dishwasher, except my mom wouldn't allow the kids to do it because she had to *wash* the dishes (not with a soapy sink, but with the scrubber) on the way to the dishwasher. It was old, and she didn't think it needed the extra strain of actually *cleaning* the dishes, so it ended up being a glorified dish steamer.

I believe that one of the most difficult concepts in parenting is how we view our children's less-than-sterling behavior. Is it something that needs attention so that our child will not be lacking in character, or is it something that is making us look like inadequate mothers? If we are disciplining our children so that we look good, our efforts are doomed from the start. When the Bible tells parents to "train a child in the way he should go," it's not referring to "train a child like a pony in your circus show and when they are old they will do cool tricks to show what a great parent you were." It means "train up this little acorn into something that has a chance to grow strong and true, that will put down deep roots and produce season after season to provide shelter for the next generation."

Discipline usually gets a bad rap in the secular press. That seems funny to me because it is that same secular media that is lamenting the passing of common courtesy amongst youngsters these days. Discipline is simply what you do to reinforce positive behavior and create a negative association with bad behavior. It is the gift we give our children that allows them to get along in this world. John and I have a few friends who, for various reasons, could not bring themselves to effectively discipline their children, being under the impression that they were doing what was loving and compassionate for said children. What they actually succeeded in doing was making the kids so rotten and ill-behaved that people *don't like them* and the children are left to wonder why. If you want to do your children a favor, teach them self-control and respect and manners and enforce these basics any way the Lord tells you to, but enforce them. Part of the joy of being a parent is raising the kind of kids other people want to be around.

Loving discipline is firm but not without compassion. Herein lies the rub, as most people who fall strongly into the compassion category cannot find the strength to balance their discipline. Most people who fall strongly into the "toe the line/cut the muster/rules and regs/straight and narrow" category cannot temper their harsh edge with love and compassion, so their discipline can all too often be embarrassing and degrading for the child. Loving discipline is never abusive, unfair, or demeaning, but always administered with respect and dignity. Whenever it's possible, explain the discipline before, affirm your love afterward. Of course this is all fine theory unless your child has just done something that has caused you to lose your ever-lovin' mind. In that case you might need to administer an "in the moment" attachment of pain and grief to the action and then explain and affirm later. I believe just a smidge of parental craziness from time to time lets your kids know that you're not a love machine; you're a human being with the capacity to lose it.

And let's admit it: We can get a little over the top when we are trying to give our kids the benefit of our experience and they are *just not listening.* We start out with such high hopes, dreams, and aspirations for our kids. We don't want them to make the same kinds of mistakes we made. If we had our way they would make *no* mistakes at all. Or, if they did, they could at least make spectacularly unique, new, fresh mistakes. Unfortunately, there aren't any of those. We are individuals, yet the issues we face as human beings are yawningly common. So our kids *are* going to mess up, and it will remind us of ourselves or someone in our family. In those moments we will probably react (rather than respond) and we *will* occasionally fail these precious people abysmally. We will be mad at ourselves. We will be frustrated with the situation. We will wish things were different. We *will* be human.

But if we keep our eye on the ball of celebrating our kids (not just accepting them), we will hit more than a few home runs when it comes to parenting. Kids will know if we are laboring to merely accept them ("Wow, I have really done something here. After all this work I have finally accepted that thou art mine offspring and as long as thou reflectest well upon me, thou art blessed") versus enjoying the calling to celebrate them ("Wow, I can't believe that I get to be your mom"). These human gifts that God has entrusted to our care are fully themselves—not who we wish they were. They have the potential for all our bad traits, all their father's bad traits, our brother's bad traits—shoot! We could probably go back four generations and find people with traits we don't like that stare back at us through our kids. The balance of that is that they have the potential for the *best* of everyone on our family tree as well.

Sometimes it takes another person's perspective to see things in your own child that might otherwise go unappreciated. I love the story Patsy Clairmont tells about the little girl in the bookstore who insisted that she sit down and read her a book. Patsy, inexplicably, did. When the mother came around the corner and saw the scene, she rolled her eyes as if to say, "Oh no, not again." Patsy said, "She told me to sit here. I think your daughter has tremendous leadership potential"—to which the exasperated mom replied, "And all this time we just thought she was bossy."

As much as John and I have loved being parents to our kids, we are constantly reminded of those who are struggling with infertility. This is one of the most difficult realities about which to find anything to celebrate *at all*. I have friends who would call every month when they would get their period and they would be wiped out emotionally with disappointment for several days. Then they would hope again, and three weeks later, cry again. The pain of childlessness is hard to wrestle with even to the point of acceptance because it seems that some women have more than enough eggs and endometrial lining to host a host of babies, and some can't even get pregnant to begin with. I can't begin to understand what that feels like. I have walked alongside friends in this journey and they have told me how agonizing it is when you want to give birth to your own offspring but cannot.

I do know that just because you cannot conceive does *not* mean that you cannot be a parent. Our friends Donna and Troy van Liere struggled with infertility for years before deciding that God must have a baby for them somewhere other than in her ovaries. Donna says that the moment she adopted her first baby girl (Gracie), the bond was instant and fierce and she knew that God had placed this child on the earth for her. They have since adopted another girl and are awaiting their third child soon. Donna and Troy cannot believe the joy that loving these babies has brought to their lives.

I was recently at an event in Estes Park, Colorado, where Steven Curtis Chapman was hosting a concert. In the middle of the evening he talked about how his teenage daughter began talking to him and his wife, Mary Beth, several years ago about the possibility of their family adopting. He told her that it was a decision that only Mary Beth could make because so much of his time was spent traveling. Mary Beth was just beginning to experience some of that "blessed quiet" that comes when the kids get a little older and self-directed. She could not imagine that adopting any child under the age of five could be a good thing! But her daughter kept persisting and eventually Mary Beth's heart opened to the idea. The Chapmans ended up adopting not one, but *three* girls from China. This literally doubled the tally of Chapman kids already hatched. Steven joked that he and his wife have set as their goal to get all the babies out of diapers before it's time for the parents to be wearing them. He sang the song he wrote about adoption called "When Love Takes You In," and I'm pretty sure that the Sniffle Factor in the audience was off the charts—probably because we who have experienced God's mercy know we have been adopted and "taken in" by the Lord, regardless of who has abandoned us in the past. Steven then brought all three of his cutie-pies on stage and let them say hello to the audience. It was so endearing to see these Asian beauties with strong Tennessee accents clinging to their dad. Steven and Mary Beth have started a ministry called Shaohannah's Hope, which helps people who want to adopt but are having trouble funding their dream. There are children for you to love. Perhaps you are the answer to a child's most fervent prayer.

Whether your struggle is to have a child or to celebrate the ones you have been given, parenting is a journey of love. I love my children, and I pray that they envision me doing the Snoopy Happy Dance because I *get* to be their mom.

if all your friends set fire to their cubicles, would you?

I feel bad about Pluto.

Not the Disney character, the planet. Well, maybe more accurately "Pluto, formerly known as a Planet."

Seems that Pluto got demoted. Just like that. The solar system downsized and poor Pluto was unceremoniously dumped from the planet list due to a meeting of leading astronomers in Prague. The International Astronomical Union stripped Pluto of its planetary status that it has held since its discovery in 1930. Talk about no appreciation for history! Talk about no respect for tenure! According to the IAU, "The decision by the prestigious international group spells out the basic terms that celestial objects will have to meet before they can be considered for admission to the elite cosmic club." Unfortunately, Pluto doesn't make the grade under the new rules for a planet: "a celestial body that is in orbit around the sun, has sufficient mass for its self-gravity to overcome rigid body forces so that it assumes a . . . nearly round shape, and has cleared the neighborhood around its orbit." Doesn't that description sound like the svelte-challenged lady in your neighborhood? You know the rather large lady from down the street who has a certain, um . . . mass, is nearly rotund, and clears the neighborhood around her orbit when she walks down the sidewalk?

To be a bona fide planet you now have to carry a certain heft. Alas, Pluto was disqualified because of its oblong orbit and was demoted to a "dwarf planet." So how weird would that be? One day you're a bona fide planet, the next day you're a dwarf. And who thinks that Disney doesn't rule this galaxy?

Anyone who's ever had a job of any kind knows how difficult and tenuous it can be. One day you're the company darling, the next day you get the news that you're no longer necessary for their orbit, or have been replaced by something that plugs into an outlet and doesn't require health benefits. Work is just that, w-o-r-k. It's actually part of the curse for the rebellion in the Garden of Eden. Adam would be destined to work the once-fruitful land and, for all the sweat that he would put into it, the ground would produce thorns. That being interpreted "you know it don't come easy." Most of us have never worked a job in landscaping though we've all felt the "thorns" that accompany any labor. That's why it's called "work." If it were all fun, then they'd call it "play." And even *that's* not totally true because some people can turn play into work—you know how certain people attach their self-esteem to any endeavor and try to prove something and just suck all the fun out of stuff? But in general, if you earn a check for it, somewhere there's going to be an element of it that requires sweat of some sort, either intellectually, emotionally, or physically. And it's hard to get results some days.

There are many of us who work to live. We go to the job, do whatever it takes to get the paycheck, in order to do what it is that we love to do. Then there are others of us who live to work. Work *is* the thing we love to do, and we would do it whether or not anyone paid us a penny for our time. The work itself is its own reward and reason enough to get up in the morning with a smile.

What's interesting to note is our human propensity for immense dissatisfaction with our employment situation—no matter what it is. There are many people who have a job and just want to be at home, and there are just as many people who are at home and would love to be back at the office. Doesn't it seem like we should declare a "Flip Flop Year" where all the dissatisfied people could switch places for a while? No matter what you're doing to earn a living, there will be days when you are just staying by the stack and keeping up with your job description. You muster all your resources and do everything you can, and what do you get? Thorns. Pain. Disappointment. Everyone's job has some thorns here and there.

I wish I had understood this principle earlier in life. I was naive enough to think that somewhere out there existed The Perfect Job where all was sweetness and light and you didn't have to deal with anything you didn't want to deal with because that would be Someone Else's Perfect Job. Reality check, please!

I have had several jobs in my lifetime. I think my first real job was babysitting, which I believe to be *the* most effective tool in preventing teen pregnancies. I spent one night as a waitress and I wasn't even allowed to interact with people. My job was to fill up the cheese crocks, and I quickly began to believe that it might not be my highest calling. I just couldn't find the filling of the cheese crocks *fulfilling*. Besides, it was port wine cheese and I was afraid that I may have violated some Baptist principle by abetting in its consumption.

One summer I worked as a census taker. My parents worried about me because I was assigned to a very large trailer park and had to ask some people who barely spoke English whether they used gas or electric heat. You would be surprised at how sensitive people can get when they think you are asking about their gas.

I was also a piano teacher in high school. I had students from the ages of five to nine, and I even held little recitals for them in the spring. I had some students who were really promising and some whose money I probably should have refunded, but compared to my friends flipping burgers and refolding clothes in retail, I was on Easy Street. When I was in college, I worked at a paint store mixing paint for contractors (I didn't really make any money working there because I ruined so many clothes while opening and closing the paint cans) and reorganizing the wallpaper books over and over and over again because women who were trying to decide on wallpaper never took out *just one* wallpaper book. Oh, no! They had to look at *all* the wallpaper books. I even tried labeling the spines so that they would know this book was ONLY FLORALS and not to bother with it if they were looking for stripes. Alas, no dice. (Did I mention that each book weighed about twenty pounds?) I found myself feeling a pinch of empathy for those workers who one day just go crazy on their customers as

I imagined myself hurling those massive wallpaper books through the plate glass window in the front of the store. I never actually did it, but there were many days I had to talk myself out of it.

So before I had to sign up for a course in anger management I quit that job and decided to sell a truly modern marvel of engineering overachievement, Rainbow Vacuum Cleaners. This was driven by my desire to *own* a Rainbow Vacuum Cleaner, the only vacuum cleaner that used water as its filter and promised to cut down on dust in our newlywed domicile. John and baby Calvin had chronic allergies and I believed that a Rainbow vacuum was our ticket out of purchasing Dimatap in gallon sizes. I wasn't really committed to making Rainbow converts worldwide, so as soon as I sold four (to family members, who still own them, by the way), I was done with that career. But I've also sold Longaberger baskets just because I wanted to own some. Perhaps this explains why there are so many Mary Kay consultants—they just want lots of makeup.

Next I tried my hand (or I guess, more accurately, my voice) at something called an "on-air personality," a radio DJ for a morning drive-time show—which is *exceedingly* difficult if you're not a morning person (you can't see me but I am raising my hand right now). We were sponsored by Burger King and Dunkin' Donuts, so Croissanwiches and lemon-filleds were considered a huge company perk.

I've been a church pianist (and been the object of others' "pianist envy"), and I am proud to say that my years on the bench have given me the ability to render "Just As I Am" about 1,000 different ways. I've also gotten so bored playing background music behind the pastor extending the incredibly long invitation even longer that I have (on occasion, and only for my own amusement—I swear it did not detract from the impassioned plea of the pastor) resorted to dropping in a few measures from such hymns of the faith as "Born to Be Wild" and "Stairway to Heaven," the latter being a perfect selection for the moment. I challenge you to listen closely to your church pianist in case he/she is doing a little extracurricular arranging in those long stretches.

So now I'm a comedian (which may be the most fun job of all time), but I can honestly say that even this one has a downside. In my current profession I must board airplanes just about every week and be subjected to the TSA New Random Security Rule of the Week and, upon awakening in a strange city, check the telephone by the bed to remember where I am. I also only take showers in the various hotel bathrooms. I know that giving up a nightly bath in my own tub sounds like a piddly sacrifice, but sometimes I cry about it. Some of you have much more difficult circumstances that you endure for the sake of your calling. So thank you, Adam and Eve. Because you blew it, the rest of us have to be working stiffs, too.

It starts with the job interview, and normally this interviewer has been trained at the Incredibly Difficult Trick Question School. So they will ask you questions like, "What do you see as your biggest weakness?" How do you answer that? "I don't have any." (Then your weakness is pride.) "Sometimes my enthusiasm gets the best of me." (Another way to say you are excitable/annoying.) Or maybe the question is, "So why did you leave your last job?" (By the way, there is no correct answer to this question. Just memorize this answer — it's as close to right as you will get: "I was looking for a growth opportunity like this one.") Plus, you're never really sure what to wear for the interview. If you outdress the HR director, you're uppity. You don't want to try too hard lest you exceed casual corporate structure, but if you undershoot and look as though you don't understand the work environment it's hard to rebound from a bad first impression. This is when it would be great to have a Wardrobe Scout Service for interviewees. For a fee they would send a scout in (maybe as a messenger service or a temp) to get the lay of the Clothes Land for you and then suggest the perfect outfit to get the job. Hey, I think there's a startup "growth opportunity" for someone here!

They also have "interview coaches" to help people overcome their tendencies to sabotage themselves in the interview process. That would have been helpful for one lady I heard about. The interviewer says to Mrs. Smith, "So tell me, do you have any other skills you think might be worth mentioning?"

"Actually yes," Mrs. Smith replied. "Last year I had two short stories published in national magazines, and I finished my first novel."

"Very impressive," the interviewer commented, "but I was thinking of skills you could apply during office hours." Mrs. Smith perked up and said, "Oh, that *was* during office hours."

So, here's a universal truth that no one really tells you, not even your "interview coach." Even if you survive the interview process and are hired, *you will face the same people who were on your last job*. The same types of people. I'm sorry to disappoint you like this, but they are e-v-e-r-y-w-h-e-r-e. That's why sitcoms like *The Office* and cartoons like Dilbert are popular. They take the types of people you encounter in every work situation, exaggerate their flaws, and all of a sudden you're laughing because *you know these people.* The names may be different, but that's pretty much where the differences end. So if you are leaving your last job to get away from the people you didn't like, bummer. You will see them again. I promise. The trick is to find a job that is so fulfilling to you personally that you can "decorate" your coworkers, or maybe just paper over them with all your award recognition certificates.

And let's be completely honest here; there just *are* some jobs that are easier than others, such as:

- Ice cream tasters, especially for Häagen Dazs.
- Vanna White's job on *Wheel of Fortune* (an actual Vanna White quote, "It's not the most intellectual job in the world, but I do have to know the letters").
- The guy who sings the Arabic music that's at the start of every movie these days.
- Spa tester—but, then again, it could be difficult to write the summary and review of services when you're too relaxed. It must be tough . . .
- The guy who says, "Let's get ready to rummmmmmmble."

So what distinguishes an easy job from a difficult job? If you hate your job, you're going to think it's hard. If you hate your work environment, it's going to be hard. If you feel unappreciated or unvalued, you will want to be somewhere else. If you're not challenged, you're going to be bored and the clock will crawl. And it's no wonder that we feel more exhausted by our jobs these days. Consider these stats from *Take Back Your Time: Fighting Overwork and Time Poverty in America*:

- We're putting in longer hours on the job now than we did in the 1950s, despite promises of a coming age of leisure before the year 2000.
- In fact, we're working more than medieval peasants did, and more than the citizens of any other industrial country.
- Mandatory overtime is at near record levels, in spite of a recession.
- On average, we work nearly nine full weeks (350 hours) LONGER per year than our peers in Western Europe do.
- Working Americans average a little over two weeks of vacation per year, while Europeans average five to six weeks. Many of us (including 37 percent of women earning less than $40,000 per year) get no paid vacation at all.
- The Girl Scouts recently introduced a "Stress Free" merit badge for today's harried young girls.

Can you believe that we work about nine more weeks per year than Western Europeans? Imagine what you would do with nine weeks of vacation built into your calendar. We are wealthy in income but impoverished in time resources. It is of the essence that we examine why we are working, and possibly more important, why we are working so *much*. No wonder we are burned out and can no longer find much motivation for our chosen field.

I saw Anderson Cooper (of CNN) give an interview recently, and in it he responded to a question regarding the best advice his mother (Gloria Vanderbilt) ever gave to him. He responded that she advised him to follow his bliss and the money would come. I don't know if that would work for everyone, but he had a dream to be a reporter and he now anchors each weeknight with his own news show. I don't know what your "bliss" might be, but I urge you to find a calling in life and attach it to your work. This kind of attitude readjustment allows us to see even the most mundane tasks as meaningful.

Perhaps the simplest way to begin to reframe our work life is to take some direction from the Word of God. Whether you have a job and wish you didn't, or don't have one and wish you did, or if you wish you had different people to work with or report to, the dailyness of your workplace can become a mental drag if you don't choose to see it as a place of purpose and mission. The Bible gives us clear principles regarding whatever labor we undertake:

- Whatever your hand finds to do, do it as unto the Lord. (Colossians 3:23)
- Once you set your hand to the plow do not turn back. (Luke 9:62)
- Honor those in authority over you. (Romans 13:1)
- Do unto others as you would have them do unto you. (Matthew 7:12)

These scriptural principles allow us to see that we are working for more than a paycheck, that we are committed to endurance and excellence in any undertaking, and that our Real Boss doesn't inhabit the corner office, but has it all in His hands.

if time waits for no man, it certainly takes women for a ride

One of the most dreaded phrases in my childhood used to be, "You aren't old enough yet." This was the case when I wanted to wear certain things (blush, mascara, go-go boots), go various places (to the movies, to a friend's house to spend the night, to the communion table — the grape juice and broken saltines look so irresistible when you're five years old), or do slightly dangerous things (own a pet, ride a motorcycle, date). What I wouldn't give to hear that phrase one more time applied to me for *any* reason. It seems I'm old enough for just about anything now, and way past eligible for many things except for the Red Hat Society. I'm still too young to get into that organization. But I am also still too young for annual colonoscopies or an AARP discount. So it's a mixed bag.

They say your age is just a number on your driver's license. But that's not really true, is it? Mainly because your age is not printed on your driver's license, just your birthdate, which then becomes a math problem if you can't remember how old you actually are. Then you must do a subtraction of the year you were born from the current year (that's assuming you can remember what the current year is, and don't ask me in the first quarter of any new year). And you can't tell your age by looking at that picture, either. The woman in the square photo on your driver's license resembles someone you hope you don't look like five years from now, and she is definitely having a bad hair day. Could that woman really be *you*? It's like Erma Bombeck said, "When you start looking like your passport photo it's time to go home."

Age (and the various expensive methods of staving off its effects) is not just an American pastime, it's become our cultural obsession. Youth is worshiped or dismissed, depending on who's talking and how much money they have to throw at the issue. The newspapers will sum it all up with a headline about celebrities like, "50 is the new 30." Well sure it is—for *them*, with their weekly facials and plastic surgeons on speed dial, trainers at their beck and call, chefs that prepare "egg white only" omelettes, stylists that shop for them to make sure their wardrobe is very *now*, personal assistants to do all their errands, and a masseuse to massage away any stress they have time to encounter between their hair appointments. But for us regular Janes who get our own Starbucks and fill our own gas tanks, age is just a subtraction problem on our license, and our photo in the little square clearly transmits, "50: It's the new 53."

You occasionally hear your more positive friends (read

"tragically disconnected to reality") say, "You know, you're as young as you feel!" Really? If that's true my age fluctuates wildly during the course of a day. Get up, catch a glimpse of myself in the mirror: feel 30. Put on glasses and look again: feel 60. I felt a little younger a couple of weeks ago when John and I went to a concert at Chastain Amphitheater. Earth, Wind & Fire was playing hit after hit from the seventies and eighties. Based solely on my mental flashbacks I was feeling all of seventeen. Based on how my feet felt as they were swelling in my strappy sandals and my ability to afford tickets to see that particular show, I was feeling every year I've accumulated. It averaged out to be somewhere around 35. I went with the feeling.

I feel my age when I can't see things (if the object is too close to my eyes or if the print font is smaller than 12). I feel my age when I realize that practically all the restroom stalls are too far away from wherever I am. It's not that they've been relocated, it's just that my perception of the imminent danger of the distance has changed. I call it the "Horse to the Barn Syndrome." If you've ever ridden a horse you will note that when the horse recognizes the barn is in range, he will begin to gallop faster and faster in the home stretch. You can try to pull back on the reins, but the horse has seen the barn and the ride is as good as over. This is how my brain processes the restroom stall. As soon as I have an unoccupied stall on my radar my body moves faster and faster hoping I can make it because my "horse" has seen the "barn." If you're under the age of forty, you can laugh all you want. But just wait. And if you're over fifty, you can laugh, but you might leak.

I've also noticed that I'm inching closer to that old-lady-makeup phenomenon called The Line of Demarcation. It sounds like a relief map topography feature ("here at The Line of Demarcation is where the Louisiana Purchase ends"). It's that point where the face makeup stops at the chin line and there is a definite difference in the two colors of the skin, sorta like one of those commercials for deck sealer—you can tell which part has been treated and which hasn't. But really this makeup *faux pas* is more like an unspoken declaration: "I will no longer pay attention to any part I can't see well, and if you can see this line, you're too close." It's a line that causes aging women a measure of confusion because once we start down the chin line to blend it, where do we stop? In the curve where the chin becomes the neck? And what about the line *there*? Do we just continue spreading our foundation down to where our skin meets our clothing? And how do we get all that makeup off our clothes? And who wants to use that much foundation for the sake of "blending" anyway? It's just the right amount of bother to make me sympathetic to The Line of Demarcation. The next time you see it on a woman imagine that she is merely trying to keep her clothes clean.

Men don't have to worry about such things. It's unfair that men don't seem to age as dramatically as women. John turned fifty this year and my teenage daughter's friends were discussing his upcoming birthday. One of them said, "But Elyse, your dad is hot. He's like an Armani model." It's true, too. He looks better than ever. None of Elyse's friends refers to me and any models in the same sentence. I'm not bitter. Really.

Age *is* somewhat about how young you feel. This would explain the discrepancy between the way some women *should* dress and the way they *do* dress. Not that I'm the Fashion Police, but if you are over the age of thirty and you are looking for your style tips in *Teen People* you may be in some serious denial. On the other hand, if you're under fifty and you are still wearing a jumper you got in 1986 or anything from "Flashdance," or if you are a homeschool mom and have a bow in your hair, it's time to visit Goodwill. Not to buy! To drop off! This is the reason organizational experts advise us to purge our wardrobes from time to time because it keeps us from dressing like the women we *used* to be. Some of my friends think they're being frugal by hanging on to clothes for decades, but my guess is that they are too lazy to try stuff on. I don't advocate that we enslave ourselves to fashion, but at least try to keep current in an age-appropriate way. Your children and friends will silently thank you.

Just like you can't always tell the numbers on the odometers of some gently driven vehicles, not all women age at the same rate. Plus, some women get their "odometers" turned back at the plastic surgeon's office. This is illegal in the car business, by the way. Now I'm not saying anything about plastic surgery in general, because I think it's fine to do everything you can afford to look your best, but there are Good Lifts and Lifts Gone Wrong. If, after your surgery, people say, "Wow, you look great. Have you been on vacation? Did you lose weight? Did you change your hair?" implying that the surgery was so subtle that they can't really put their finger on why you look better, then that could qualify as a Good

Lift. However, if after your surgery people say, "Hey, we've got a bet as to whether or not your eyelids shut all the way at night," that might qualify as a Lift Gone Wrong. General Lift Advice: Never let them pouf your lips beyond the tip of your nose, stitch skin that used to be near your nose up in your hairline, or inject botulism spores into your forehead. And it's a good idea to donate more to missions than you give to your surgeon in a calendar year. Other than that, have a great time.

Even if you can't afford surgery, at a certain age you start throwing pennies (dollars, second mortgages) into the fountain of youth, hoping for a little reprieve from the hands of time. Cosmetics companies know this full well and aptly label just about every product on the shelf "anti-aging." I know they mean well, but doesn't it sound like we are vehemently opposed to the very idea of getting older? Like aging is some sort of disease instead of a natural process? And if it sounds like the product has miraculous qualities, all the better. I read about a product called Crème de La Mer, a moisturizer that sells for about a kajillion dollars an ounce (slight exaggeration, but if you haven't had a car payment in a while, it's close to the amount of your last car payment). And more than the cost of an ounce of Beluga Caviar. (Speaking of which, why *is* caviar so expensive? Is it hard to get the fishies to give up their eggs? Do the mama fish get belligerent at having their offspring harvested? Does it taste all that great? Or is it just one of those things that you do to prove that you have money to burn?) This Crème de la Mer's key ingredient is the "miraculous broth" of "fermented sea kelp" (insert your own gagging noise here), and it's supposed to be The End All of All Creams. Now what if someone on the beach came up to you and said, "Hey lady, I've got some sea kelp that I've been keeping in a barrel so that it could ferment awhile. I stuck it in a jar with some other slimy stuff and I would appreciate it if you'd reach into your purse and give me $100 for it. How does that sound to you?" We'd be reaching in our purse, all right, but it would be for the mace spray. But change the setting of the same spiel to a department store and let celebrities endorse it and use words like "miraculous properties" and "amazing results," and you've got women ponying up and spending their yearly shoe budget for an ounce of the stuff.

Purely out of research for this book (cough, cough) I went on eBay and bought some sample sizes of the eye and face cream. As soon as it arrived I used miniscule amounts (you have to make it last) on my eyes and face and went to bed like a kid on Christmas Eve so it could hurry up and work its magic overnight. The next morning I rushed to the mirror to see what miracles fermented sea kelp could do in a mere eight hours and, to my surprise, I still looked the same. Slightly more hydrated, but not miraculously younger or firmer or more fabulous. (I might call it "dewey" but isn't "dewey" normally followed by the words "decimal system"?) And I do believe the sea kelp may be cultivating a bumper crop of some random barnacle growth beneath my chin.

We have become so obsessed with our fear of wrinkles and anything that even hints that our chronological age is inching up that we have started using military vocabulary to describe our battle with the effects of aging. We're now "defending" against aging—against the marauding avenger cells called The Free Radicals (doesn't that sound like the people you knew from college who were the liberated, highly verbal, opinionated ones?). But these cells that are trying to overthrow youth in female bodies will not be met without a fight! No siree! No Free Radicals will be allowed to form their coalitions, causing crow's feet and age spots. What are "age spots" anyway? Like your body just got tired of storing that extra melanin somewhere inside and decided it could no longer evenly distribute it in the form of freckles, so it got lazy and deposited it all in a single half inch? According to the Cosmetics Warlords you do *not* want any of those Free Radical cells to bunch up together and create a cluster. If they gain power and take over, it's the Aging Coup, and you don't want that to happen. In that case you would need "antioxidants" (are these chemicals "against oxes"?) to come in and bust up the Free Radicals' party. This would explain why women are tense all the time. Their antioxidants are performing counterterrorist ops to liberate their skin from the Wrinkle Jihad.

You could also choose to get your face professionally cared for by an esthetician who will study your skin under a very bright magnifying lamp. She has attended a special "esthetician school" (to study "esth"?) where the primary drill is to refrain from shrinking back in horror at the size of your pores or the dirt contained therein that she can see because of the intense, bright, hot magnifying light. When you look at your face in your mirror, it is as if you are seeing your face on a 13-inch TV screen. When the facial lady fires up her high-powered MagLamp, she is looking at your face on the equivalent of the movie screens in your local movie theater. Too much information.

According to the American Osteopathic College of Dermatology (and who is gonna argue with them?) you cannot, I repeat *cannot*, change your pore size. They say that it's genetically predetermined and that your pores are adult size when you reach puberty. They can appear larger when they are "impacted" with "sebaceous material or bacteria." (This would be a dermatological euphemism for "your face is incredibly dirty.") But this is where a facialist can help you. She can get out her Super Duper Magnifying Lamp and do to you what your mother told you never to do to yourself: squeeze the D-O-G out of your face. And it hurts. So much that you are relieved that your eyes are covered with the soothing cucumber pads as they absorb your tears. She'll also cluck and say things like, "How long has it been since you had your last facial?" implying that it's your lack of attention and dollars that is making your pores larger. After she spends ten minutes scraping the "sebaceous material" out of your "congested zone" she will put some sort of soothing treatment on it to make sure that when you walk out of her room you won't scare the next client.

I prefer to think of my pores as tiny caves where the outer opening is larger than the inside; if I could just rid myself of my top layer of skin, I could reduce the size of the cave openings. Makes sense, right? If that's your feeling, you could sign up for the facial equivalent to sandblasting known as microdermabrasion. For a fee they will pelt your face with millions of particles of sand while simultaneously sucking the loose skin into a Dustbuster the size of

an ink pen. I have no idea how the physics of that works — how
the same thing that is hurtling the particles at you could be vacu-
uming them up concurrently. That just doesn't make sense — like
saying that your leaf blower and your vacuum cleaner could be the
same unit at the same time. But they claim that this blasting thins
your skin out and the sucking motion stimulates collagen production. And all this time we thought we could do that by applying
pricey creams. Silly us.

I've noticed of late that my skin is morphing into someone
else's. I used to have incredibly dry skin around my nose, down-
right flakey on both sides. So what does my nose decide to do in
the past couple of years? All of a sudden it starts to release all the
oil it's been so stingily hoarding all my life and make the middle of
my face so reflective that my friends can check the application of
their lipstick after dinner. I used to try to give it a hint with astrin-
gents and oil-control products that would communicate, "Your oil
is not welcome in this spot. I know that I wished for it for years,
but you're too late and you're sending too much!" Like when Bette
Midler's character in the movie *Beaches* wants the apartment super
to send up the heat and it takes awhile to get up to her apartment
through the old furnace pipes. I am now trying the approach that
usually worked with my kids — reverse psychology. If I wanted
them to do something I forbade it. ("No more making beds!" "You
cannot fold the clothes!" "Don't ever cut that grass again, young
man!") It worked for a while. So I figure that my nose can't be that
smart, right? I am now moisturizing it like it is the driest patch
on my body. It's like supply-side economics. I hope it will think,

"Hey, there's plenty of oil up there; let's shut down the supply." So far, it isn't working. But it took fifteen years for the face to get the message to "send more oil, it's dry and flaky up here," so maybe my super is a slow mover.

No matter what your age as represented by your driver's license or birth certificate, your health is what matters, right? You can look like a twenty-five-year-old on the outside and be ninety on the inside. Your habits and lifestyle are a better predictor of what some health experts call your "real age." They have a test for it! (And you know how we chicks love little tests.) You can log on to the website at www.realage.com and go through the list of questions about your medical history, your family history, your habits, your nutrition, and your stressors and, voila! Their little program can tell you what your "real age" is. And it's little things like daily flossing and whether or not you talk on your cell phone while driving that can ratchet your "real age" higher.

But what does your age really represent? Days and nights spent living your life, coming through a myriad of experiences that sometimes seem mind-numbingly monotonous, only to be interrupted by life-altering surprises and unforeseen tragedies. Your age reflects years of (hopefully) collected wisdom. I have a theory that all this hard-won wisdom must begin to show on your body — it most often settles in the midsection. So you can observe women in your everyday life and determine which of them may be rich in wisdom by noting the size of their "Wisdom Waist" — which turns out to be a great canvas for decoration, by the way. I hear women say that they don't wear belts because they don't have a tiny waist. Nonsense. This vast canvas of the Wisdom Waist is practically screaming to be adorned. Do not hide your wisdom! Get a big ol' belt and bling your wisdom up!

Your age also represents mounds of memories. You've exchanged some of the energy of youth for them, but the higher the number on your birthday card, the more wealth you have in your little treasure trove of reminiscences.

John and I know a couple who have been friends to John and his family for years. Charlie and Nora served on staff at the church where John spent his high school and college years, and their influence in his life is inestimable. We have stayed in touch with them, visiting them whenever we've gone back to Mississippi to visit John's family. I was always struck by the way Charlie and Nora were so devoted to each other and their family, and how their genuine love for God always worked its way out into the way they loved and cared for others.

A few years back Charlie was driving home from his daughter's house in New Orleans. She had just given birth to one of their grandchildren, and Charlie had left Nora there to head back to Jackson on a rainy night. In an instant his car left the road and came to rest, but not before an object from the back of the car hit him in the back of his head and caused a very severe brain injury.

In the first days following the accident it was hard to tell if Charlie was going to survive. The doctors told Nora that the trauma was so forceful that most of the synapses that allowed the left and right sides of his brain to communicate with each other were destroyed, and that if he survived at all, they could give no prognosis on his level of recovery mentally and physically. This was unthinkable to any of us in regard to a man who was always the driest wit in the room and a proud prankster. And a man who loved so many so well. It didn't sound good.

As days turned into weeks and months, Charlie did survive. He had broken just about everything that could be broken and went through months of rehab to learn to walk and talk again. If you sit down to talk with him now you will see flashes of the old Charlie that show his cockeyed view of life and make you laugh. But the thing that struck me as I sat in their living room a few months ago and listened to Nora explain things to Charlie is that *she has now become his memory*, because most of the life he knew before was wiped out in the moment of the accident. John and I talked about it in the car as we left their house, that the memories you accrue over your lifetime become such a part of the definition of your existence and what a loss it is when you can't find them anymore.

I would imagine that this is one of the most devastating parts of having a parent with Alzheimers—that their memory, their sense of personal and family history, gradually leaves without saying good-bye. And you are left trying to explain to them who they used to be and who you all were collectively. All that to say this: When you think of your age and how you long for a time when you were younger and faster and it didn't hurt to bend over, just try to imagine which part of your treasure chest of memories you'd trade for your youth.

The only time I read fiction books is when we go to the beach on vacation. I don't know if I don't make the time during the rest of the year or if I'm just not that into the genre, but when I have an engaging book I have a hard time finding a place to stop because I want to find out how the story turns out. I feel like that about my life. I want to know where the story goes. I don't want to get stuck on any single chapter and keep experiencing that same period in the story over and over again. Time is moving forward. My age is moving forward. My health is moving forward (well, okay, backward). How foolish to think that I could freeze myself in any one frame and not miss the life happening in real time. What a waste of precious time and energy. In our culture, age is viewed as some kind of disease that, if we just keep treating it, might be defeated or go away altogether. Like we can somehow push back the edges of mortality. The only thing we're pushing back is the edges of our acceptance of the gifts of time and the physical limitations that make the interior gifts more precious.

So you've got a year or two on your friends. So you've got a wrinkle or two. So your hair is changing color and your body is giving you fits. No matter. Age is a gift from the hand of God. Any measure of health to enjoy your age is a gift from God. The memories you've made along the way are precious and priceless. Thank God for every year He's given you.

if someone's in a wormhole, skip the decorating advice

The rule is this: If the phone rings after midnight, it's not good news. Ed McMahon never knocks on your door with the Prize Patrol after Leno signs off. The only communication you receive after midnight is along the lines of:

"We're so sorry to inform you . . ."

"Would this be the next of kin?"

"There's been a horrible accident."

"Mom, could you come down here, they're only allowing me one phone call."

And suddenly your world is flipped upside down and you find yourself in a dark, slimy, cold wormhole. You just want to wake up and find that it's a bad dream. But when you do wake up, there are people you recognize and they all seem to be having the same dream that you are. But there is now no connection to anything you felt in the moment before you answered that phone, and you are definitely awake, and it's not a dream at all. This is your new reality.

Into every life there will come circumstances that cataclysmi-cally quake your soul. They try your faith. They make you feel as though the world should stop spinning, but it doesn't. You've lost your footing and your mooring, and the fact that the world is still orbiting the sun just makes you dizzier. You're trying to claw your way out of the wormhole, but you can't see which way is up, and all the digging in the dirt is just making you exhausted. You run on fumes, because things still need to be done, but inside you feel hollow, tired, angry, resigned, bitter, accepting, worried, guilty, sad, mad, and useless — and that's all in a five-minute span.

You don't want to deal with it. You definitely don't want to accept it. You just want the world to go back to the way it was five minutes before that phone rang. Is that so much to ask? It seems like a simple request. And if you just had a time machine or a flux capacitor, or anything else on the SciFi Channel, you would gladly give all the money in your bank account for a ride in that machine.

But there are some situations that just cannot be decorated.

A few years back I was talking with a friend of mine whose wife died of cancer. He was asking me how my life was going, and I related a few of our family's financial challenges. He point-blank asked me how much money it would take for me to feel like my problem was solved. I hemmed and hawed, mentally tabulating how much it would take, and I answered him with what I thought was an adequate amount. He looked at me, smiling the smile of wisdom that comes through hard experience, and replied, "Anita, if you've got a problem that can be fixed with money, you really don't have a problem, do you?" I felt the hot flush of embarrassment in my cheeks, realizing that all the money in the world could not bring his wife back.

I vividly remember one evening after my mom, dad, and I had been out looking at houses, trying to find a place to call home after relocating to Virginia from Texas. When we pulled into our apartment complex in Arlington the manager was waiting for us on the front steps with the news that family members had been trying to get in touch with us all day. My mom stepped into the phone booth to make the call back home, and I'll never forget seeing her nod her head and slump to the floor. My dad rushed to her to pick up the phone and finish the conversation. The news was that her youngest brother had been brutally murdered in his own home. It was a phone call that sent us all into shock, incredulity, and deep sorrow.

John and I have had the dark privilege of walking through soul-shaking calamities with many friends over the years. I think of David and Linda who had a son, Garrett, a beautiful boy who was in our church children's choir. He was smart and sweet and loving and had pretty severe asthma all his life. Because he was their only child Linda and David were very protective of Garrett and showered him with love and affection—but not to the point of turning him into a spoiled brat. He had a great head on his shoulders, he loved God and loved other people, and all indicators pointed to him growing up to be a fine young man.

One hot summer day when he was ten years old he was out playing with his best friend in the yard. He came into the house and was laboring to breathe because of his asthma, and within a matter of minutes he said to Linda, "Mom, my chest *really* hurts." And with that he passed out, stopped breathing, and was, for all intents and purposes, dead before he arrived at the hospital.

He was Medi-vac'd to Washington, DC, to the children's hospital there, and we drove up to be with David and Linda and their family. When it became apparent after three brain scans that there was no chance of Garrett recovering, his parents were forced to watch their precious baby be disconnected from life support. I remember seeing Linda through the glass window as she and David took a bowl filled with water and a wash cloth and gently washed the face of their only child and kissed his cheek, laid their heads on his chest, and said good-bye. Being a mother of young children myself, I could not imagine her feelings in that moment, but I prayed for her beyond the edges of my imagining to the place where she was, where she had fallen down the wormhole. Her new reality would never resemble anything she had known before.

I watched my friend over the next weeks and months as she fought for her own sanity and tried to find a way to live without her child, the light of her life. The new reality was harsh, the landscape barren. Linda and David were somehow able to beat the odds of most couples who lose a child and leaned more toward each other rather than growing apart and blaming each other. They are still in love; they still have their faith intact. But their world has never been the same.

Such soul quakes cause even the strongest in their faith to question how these horrible things can come into our lives with no warning. Why do the good suffer? You can ask Job. He lost it all and God gave it back to him. My question is, Why would Job take it all back again? It seems like an awful gamble to risk that kind of anguish again.

There is a single diamond that exists in Scripture that we would love to hand to people when they have fallen down the wormhole. This diamond is verse 28 in Romans chapter 8, where Paul tells us that we know all things work together for good for those who love the Lord and are called according to His purpose. The problem is this diamond cannot be transferred from one person to another person. It's a treasure that can only be mined in the dark by the person who is trying to fight their way out of the hole. And only those who have been there can imagine how long it takes to find this truth in the dark.

The problem for those of us who witness the suffering is that we are well intentioned and want to help people climb out of the dark place. But we have no knowledge of where they are in the hole or how to direct them to the exit. Everyone's journey back into the world of the living is unique, and nothing we can say will change their new reality. But we can offer love and presence and the assurance that we will be there whenever they are able to come out.

There are a variety of practical things you can do while someone is in the dark place. The trick is to observe and fulfill needs without being asked. Because that's one of the cruelties of the darkness: You can't decide whether to breathe in or out or whether to stand up or sit down. So any offer of help that's wrapped in a decision that needs to be made seems rather overwhelming. When we are near a person who's in the dark, it's hard to see exactly what they need, but we can try. We can water the flowers, mow the grass, polish the shoes for the funeral. Little things done with great love. And if we are very blessed, when it's our turn to learn the lessons of the dark places and search for the diamond of Romans 8:28 ourselves, another kind soul will be there to offer us help without asking and a prayer beyond the edges of their own imagination.

Chapter 12

if you can't decorate it, lose it

Used to be, if you wanted to know things about people you had to hire a private detective. It is a cliché of film noir. Beautiful girl walks into gumshoe's office, gives a tale of woe, and secures his services for the gathering of information. Or else you could listen in on something called the "party line." There are many young people who think this "party line" is a 900 number you might call, but it was actually the main source of information where we lived out in the country. Several neighbors on a rural route would share one telephone line and, if you were really good at picking up the phone at the right time, you could listen in to the neighbors' conversations and get the 411 on what was going on. Some people (who lack imagination) would call this eavesdropping, but we just called it good reporting skills. But no more. Now we all have private telephone lines so we have to get our information elsewhere.

In the age of 24-hour television and web search engines we have a never-ending barrage of info about people and their life stories. This development has made us all amateur detectives. If you want to, it's now possible to find out just about anything about anybody. You can Google 'em (so prevalent is the use of this search engine that it is now an official verb in the dictionary) and then read about them to your heart's content. We even have channels on cable totally devoted to biographies. We have the stars on A&E, *E True Hollywood Stories* (is anything "true" in Hollywood?), *Driven* and *Behind the Music* on VH1 (which always includes a ride to the top of the music biz, an addiction, and a recovery to a better life). Even one of the sports channels has its own biography series called *Beyond the Glory* (they're all pretty much the same: deprived childhood, supportive momma or grandmother, raw talent, *Sports Illustrated* covers, millions in signing bonuses, happy agents). There are common elements that the producers of those TV shows are looking for: their childhood influences, the life events that determined their course, obstacles they've overcome, accomplishments, and life disappointments. They call these "backstories" — the action that happened before you tuned in and were aware that this actress/musician/sports star/model even existed. They show high school yearbook photos and conduct interviews with relatives and childhood friends trying to figure out the elements that led to their eventual triumph or demise.

What do you suppose a television producer would choose to include in *your* made-for-TV biography? Would they talk about your heartbreaking injury that ended your baton-twirling career? Perhaps they would highlight your brief stint in rehab for your adolescent addiction to McDonalds French fries, or the fact that your mom had to work two jobs to pay for your orthodontist.

The backstory of your life may not seem to be TV-worthy. It may have a series of wrong turns, a smattering of debilitating events, a few points at which you faced a fork in the road and simply could not choose which way to go, so life chose for you. And you might still be lying in the middle of that road just praying for someone to save you, to tell you that you haven't done irreparable damage. In fact, you might even feel like this is your current purpose: to be a monument to what has happened to you, a testament to your own ability to mess things up, or to wallow in what life has done to you. But no one is simply the sum of the things that have happened to them. You are more than a monument to your past—the mess ups or the triumphs. You can't afford to internalize the bad news when you're feeling down or believe your press packet when things are great. Dolly Parton, discussing a standout moment in her life, a bronze statue of her in the middle of her hometown of Pigeon Forge, Tennessee, said that her father always helped her to keep perspective on such honors. "Dolly," he said, "to your fans that statue might be some sort of idol, but to the pigeons, it's just another outhouse." (To be on the safe side, resist any tendency to become a monument to what has happened to you—good or bad.)

I dare you to try a little experiment: Listen to yourself for three days. Just the same way you would keep a food diary (a hideous idea, by the way), take a little notepad around with you for three days and summarize the conversations you have and just notate in the margin when you reread it "P" for positive comments about life or "N" for negative comments about life. I think it would really surprise you to find out just what the ratio of "N" to "P" would be. That number might quadruple if we could flag the thoughts that play in our heads all day ("I'm not pretty, I'm such an idiot, why do I always do that? What is wrong with me? Everybody's life has got to be easier than mine"). The Proverbs tell us, As a man thinks in his heart, so is he. We could regenderize it for ourselves to say, "as a woman thinks in her heart (in her head—the internal conversation that forms the thoughts that form our character which leads to choices that result in actions that add up to a life), so is she."

Reinhold Niebuhr wrote a powerful prayer, part of which has become the mainstay of 12-Steppers everywhere.

God grant me the serenity to accept the things I cannot change,
The courage to change the things I can,
And the wisdom to know the difference.

It's that last line of "wisdom" that makes the whole issue of knowing what is "loseable" and what is "up for decoration" possible. It is wisdom that peers through the lens of life and helps us rightly categorize what is a candidate for courageous feats of change and those things that must remain fixed in the acceptance column. I have spent various portions of my life decidedly outside the "wisdom to know the difference" mode, desperately trying to change things that I couldn't and avoiding changing the things that I could. Paul talks about "fighting the good fight," and I know he means "to have fought well" but could one actually be fighting a "bad fight"? Of course we can. We can spend our life energy *fighting all the wrong things.* If you are fighting your reality, not fighting to make it better, but fighting to make it *not be yours* right now, then you are engaged in the wrong battle. If you are not accepting where you are so that you can chart a path to where you know you need to go, you are not fighting the right fight.

Then again, some things weren't meant to be fought at all. Some things were meant to be released. *Control,* for instance. Isn't it most every woman's favorite losing battle?

Because I have to get on planes to get to where people are who may need to laugh, you could say that I spend a fair amount of time in airports. I happened to be flying the day the terrorists were arrested in Britain with the plot to blow up planes over the Atlantic, and the immediate security response was to ban anything remotely resembling a liquid, including all mascaras, lip glosses, lip sticks, perfumes . . . you know the drill. I saw the news alert before I left my hotel room and was able to move my potential offenders to my checked baggage, but I was amazed at the sheer volume of cosmetics—expensive $20 lip glosses and $40 bottles of their custom matched foundations—in the trash. It could have been declared a day of National Makeup Mourning. I feel that it might have been a conspiracy on the part of cosmetics manu-facturers to cause a temporary upswing in the market due to the numbers of items that had to be replaced.

It was another one of those times when you become painfully aware that we are not in control of pretty much anything. I think that the reason a lot of people are white-knuckled fliers is because the very act of flying in an airplane reveals how a perceived lack of control disturbs us. When we are near the ground we think we have more control. I have a friend who will comment as the plane descends to around 1000 feet, "I think I could jump from here." But we are acutely aware that there is someone else (by that I mean someone we don't know personally) who is flying the plane. But I don't really see the difference between being flown around by an unknown captain and getting in a cab in San Francisco (where Elyse and I spent a good four miles bumping our heads on the cab ceiling as our driver was going WAY TOO FAST over the hilly streets), because I didn't really know THAT driver, either.

I think we have to understand on some level that control is illusory. It does not exist, particularly in the areas of hormones and hair. We have precious little ability to control either of those. We want to control them, but they defy our best efforts. We throw products and pharmaceuticals at them, yet they mock us in their insubordination. And it seems our most advanced gains in technology only conspire to keep us off balance and feeling out of control. Computer viruses can come invade our information cache and crash the hard drive. You can put up all the security systems, virus definitions, and firewalls, and it can prevent some of it, but occasionally something worms its way through and you are left without access to the information you need.

I recently spent a few hours in the waiting room of the hospital's surgical unit. I brought my laptop to do some work while waiting and I was struck by the uniformity of the surroundings as all the other waiting people had the same hospital-issue clear plastic bag for the patient's clothing and belongings. As it was a clear bag you could see an array of different undergarments, shirts and blouses, socks and shoes. It's an interesting responsibility to have to hold someone's clothes. It means that they went into the surgery with their skin intact and that terrible hospital gown, and will emerge some hours later with wounds and scars and pain medication, and a list of things to do or not do over the next 24 hours. My mother was having her gall bladder out (now she doesn't have "the gall" to do the things she used to — I know it's corny, I couldn't resist), and they no longer do the massive incision from side to side. This surgery is now routinely laproscopic, or as my friend Wayne says, "a piece of cake." The truth is that whenever they open any un-God-made hole in your body, it's serious. When you are wheeled into that surgical suite and they put you out, believe me, you are surrendered to a state of total noncontrol. You aren't even allowed to keep your plastic bag of clothes with you. It reminds us of the uncontrollable elements in this thing called Life.

There is another area of our lives that will never be changed if we refuse to lose it. It's the mother of all problems, as in, "Houston we have a problem." No, it's bigger than the danger to Apollo 13. The problem is serious, life-threatening. In fact, it's deadly. This problem is sin. Failure to meet God's standard of right-ness. Our complete inability to make ourselves holy, to clean ourselves up, to make a mucked-up reality right again. We can spend our lives trying to decorate it — dress it up, call it something else, get therapy to unknot it — but the only solution is to LOSE IT. Some things just require a total loss. I don't think any of us would follow our dog around the neighborhood on the morning walk with our pooper scooper and keep those stinky pieces so that we could try to make some sort of decoration out of them. That's just gross. But that's a pretty accurate picture of what we're tempted to do with our sin. We keep holding onto it and trying to find some sort of "psychological sequins" to pass it off as something less offensive than it is. In the end it may *look* better, but it was never meant to be held onto in the first place. It just stinks.

That's why Jesus came, so we wouldn't have to keep trying to silk purse a sow's ear. Jesus didn't come to make bad people good, but to make dead people alive. He loves you and came to give you forgiveness and set you free to *live your life*, to dance in celebration of the difficult times that have made you stronger, the wonderful times that have made you a pile of memories, the uneventful times that have made you take notice of simple things and become attuned to the rhythm of life.

Life—your life—is The Party to which you're invited. You can choose to stay away (denial), show up but choose not to dance (acceptance), or show up and dance 'til you break your strap on your shoes (celebrate). The latter means refusing to sit out a number. Dancing to every song, be it a slow dance, boogie, Macarena, electric slide, line dance, tango, salsa, dirge, or swing. At different times in your life they'll play them all. Dance them all, and don't worry about the steps; they'll come to you.

Celebration is more a state of mind than an event, and I believe that anyone can learn to be a celebrator, even if the celebratory gene isn't in your DNA or wasn't expressed in your growing-up environment. I tell my kids if they see a trait in someone else that they admire, especially one they don't have much experience with, just act like that person. Don't wonder why they do what they do, just do it, and it may become apparent in the doing of it why that thing is so needful in your life. Paul said, "Imitate me as I imitate Christ." Don't worry if you're imitating badly; just take that thing on as if it were yours and it just may become so.

You may be familiar with the story of Joni Eareckson Tada's life. Due to a tragic diving accident she became a quadriplegic when she was a young adult. I'm sure that she could have curled up in fetal position, disengaged from life, given up, and quite frankly, no one would have blamed her for it. We would have totally understood why she'd do that. But instead she learned to paint by holding a brush in her mouth and got married and writes books about her very real frustration, and honestly shares the pain of her limitations, which makes her more aware of the future of heaven. She decorated her reality. And she leaves me without excuse for refusing to decorate my own.

Humor me and try another little experiment. I'll even give you two days to do it 'cause you can find out a lot in just one. Pay attention to what you say to God. Even if you don't consider yourself particularly eloquent or frequent in your prayer times, you still talk to Him. What are you saying all day, when you turn your internal thoughts heavenward? Are you telling Him how appreciative you are for your very breath? For your life? You know, not the one you thought you were signing up for, but the one you actually got. The one you're in, with all its raging, glorious imperfection. It's yours. And no matter what you're saying to God about it, regardless of where you are in gaining expertise at decorating your reality, God is listening to you. He is loving and accepting you. All of heaven is pulling for you to move past acceptance to celebration, one dance step at a time.

This is your life, girl.

Lose what you must.

Learn to accept what is unchangeable.

Then decorate like crazy!

acknowledgments

I never thought I would write four books. More honestly, I didn't know if I *could*. I remember telling Terry Behimer on the first book, "What if I write and write and all I can produce is a pamphlet?" She laughed and gave me a thesaurus (and a copy of the contract with the word count highlighted). All that to say, if I'd known I was going to write more than two books I would have spread out the Thanking of All the People a little more evenly. Instead I thanked them all in books #1 through #3 and, quite frankly, I haven't met that many new, important people who are Worthy of Thanks since then. So other than the people who are involved in the creative end (Traci Mullins, Editor Without Equal; Don Pape, Former Literary Agent Returned to The Dark Side; and Terry B. mentioned above), there is the fearless crew of the NavPress Starship Enterprise who get the words spelled correctly, the covers put on, and the books in the stores. If you are anyone other than these persons, I am putting in a template here and, if you receive this book and there is a personal message for you here, you will feel better thanked. I think. (And if you did not get something special written here feel free to disguise your own handwriting and forge what you wish I'd said in the space provided below. No one will be the wiser.)

Dear _____,

I would like to express my thanks and eternal debt of gratitude for _____

_____

_____

_____.

You have been such an inspiration to me and I could not have written this book without you.

With much love and thanks,

Anita

about the author

Anita Renfroe has the spiritual gift of saying what most women *think* but are afraid to say out loud. Her potent mix of sass, edge, and humor shine through in everything she does, and her quirky take on life entertains and inspires thousands of women (and a few secure males) each year.

A comic force to be reckoned with, Anita's infectious personality, wisdom, and honesty also shine through in the books she's written, including *The Purse-Driven Life, A Purse-Driven Christmas,* and *If It's Not One Thing, It's Your Mother.* Anita is a breath of fresh air in the midst of a sometimes-too-serious world. A mom in midlife, she gets her inspiration from her amazing husband, John, her mom, Kay, and her three highly verbal children, Calvin, Austin, and Elyse. Anita gets her mail in Acworth, Georgia, but actually resides at the baggage claim carousel #1 inside Atlanta International Airport. For more information about Anita and her upcoming appearances, visit www.anitarenfroe.com.

WANT SOME PURSE-ONALITY IN YOUR LIFE?

The Purse-Driven Life

Anita Renfroe

978-1-57683-605-7
1-57683-605-3

The Purse-Driven Life isn't exactly about finding the deeper meaning of life; it's more about shifting your perspective just enough to locate the deep humor and joy waiting to be uncovered in everyday life. Anita Renfroe offers a pull-no-punches look at the life of women, exploring areas such as:

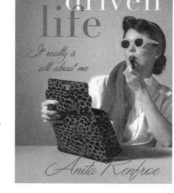

- Trying to understand our husbands
- Mammograms and their fallout
- Hoping our kids don't end up on the Jerry Springer show

This is the stuff that could drive a person crazy but won't once you look at life through Renfroe's glasses. Being a female in midlife is not for wimps; it's for discovering the humorous aspects of our shared experiences and realizing we are not alone.

> "This book will have you driving off the road, chuckling out loud in public places, and telling your girlfriends you've found the perfect gift for every woman on your gift list."
> —CAROL KENT, best-selling author of *Becoming a Woman of Influence* and *When I Lay My Isaac Down*

Visit your local Christian bookstore, call NavPress at 1-800-366-7788, or log on to www.navpress.com to purchase.

To locate a Christian bookstore near you, call 1-800-991-7747.

NAVPRESS®

BRINGING TRUTH TO LIFE
www.navpress.com

LAUGH YOUR WAY THROUGH ALL THINGS MOTHER AND DAUGHTER.

If It's Not One Thing, It's Your Mother

Anita Renfroe

978-1-57683-993-5

1-57683-993-1

Comedienne extraordinaire Anita Renfroe invites you to take a peek at motherhood through her funky specs, with hilarious insights and heartfelt stories that will encourage you to embrace your roles as a mother and daughter. Either you are one or you've got one. If you fall into both columns, you've scored double in Emotional Scrabble. How do you deal with this? Ignore it? Adjust? Cry? Return to fetal position?

Why not laugh instead? With one eye on her own mother, one eye on herself, and one eye on her own teenage daughter (okay, so she has three eyes . . .), Anita will help you laugh your way through:

- A mom's need to feed
- Smotherly love—the desire to overprotect the cubs
- Why Mother's Day is the land mine of all holidays
- The incurable Momsense-Compulsive Counsel Disorder

For less than you would spend on a box of chocolate therapy, you can get yourself some honest, hilarious, southern-fried wisdom from a chick who knows what it's like on both sides of this fence. You'll laugh, you'll cry, you'll need either Depends or an epidural. Sorta like motherhood.

Visit your local Christian bookstore, call NavPress at 1-800-366-7788, or log on to www.navpress.com to purchase.

To locate a Christian bookstore near you, call 1-800-991-7747.

NAVPRESS

BRINGING TRUTH TO LIFE

www.navpress.com

STIMULATING STUDIES FROM THE REAL LIFE STUFF FOR WOMEN SERIES.

Designed for small groups, yet just as useful for personal study, this lively, relevant, and easy-to-use Bible study series for women is based on *The Message*, the eye-opening translation by Eugene Peterson. The series provides a safe place for exploring the truths that matter, taking you where you need to go and bringing greater hope and meaning to your life.

Waking Up from the Dream of a Lifetime

978-1-57683-862-4   1-57683-862-5

Your husband isn't quite the guy you thought you married, your kids face challenges you never dreamt of, you have to work a lot more than you expected just to make ends meet, and even the bedroom wallpaper you saved up for just looks wrong. Let this Bible study help you overcome the endless disappointment.

Running Nowhere in Every Direction

978-1-57683-836-5   1-57683-836-6

To say we're busy is like saying Greenland has ice. With this Bible study and a few girlfriends who are just as wiped out but want to get somewhere too, you can link arms and begin figuring out how you can get off the treadmill.

Searching for God in a Bottomless Purse

978-1-57683-863-1   1-57683-863-3

Your spiritual life can bring you deep comfort, abiding assurance, and wisdom for living. But what about those times when your worship feels dry, prayers only bounce off the ceiling, and God seems totally unreachable? If you are ready for a faith-lift, here is some trustworthy guidance.

Peeking into a Box of Chocolates

978-1-57683-835-8   1-57683-835-8

Some temptations are more appealing than others, but all of them can pull us away from the things that really matter. This guide helps you uncover the core issues behind the temptations and then deal with them in God's forgiving grace.

Visit your local Christian bookstore, call NavPress at 1-800-366-7788,
or log on to www.navpress.com to purchase.
To locate a Christian bookstore near you, call 1-800-991-7747.

NAVPRESS®
BRINGING TRUTH TO LIFE
w w w . n a v p r e s s . c o m

EMPOWER YOUR GIRLFRIENDS WITH SMART NEW WAYS TO STUDY THE BIBLE.

No one promised studying the Bible would be easy, but no one said it was supposed to be all work and no play either. Join Bible teacher and author **Jen Hatmaker** as she introduces refreshing ways to learn and laugh while forming a deeper connection with God's Word.

A Modern Girl's Guide to Bible Study

978-1-57683-891-4   1-57683-891-9

Like a funny conversation between friends, this book will make you laugh out loud as it transforms the academic nature of personal Bible study into a fresh, simple format that will radically change the way you interact with Scripture forever.

Road Trip

978-1-57683-892-1   1-57683-892-7

You navigate *life* with your girlfriends, why not the Bible? Guided by Abraham, the Samaritan women, Peter, Paul, and Jesus himself, you're guaranteed the trip of a lifetime!

Tune In

978-1-57683-893-8   1-57683-893-5

You may think you've got a one-sided relationship with God, but He's in constant dialogue with us. Are you ready to tune Him in?

Girl Talk

978-1-57683-895-2   1-57683-895-1

Learn how to open up, find safe friendships, and deal with disappointments, all while studying the biblical model for unity.

Make Over

978-1-57683-894-5   1-57683-894-3

Make Over delivers rich, relevant biblical content in a fun, casual voice. It features thirty-minute devotionals in a simple six-week format that fits into any schedule.

Visit your local Christian bookstore, call NavPress at 1-800-366-7788, or log on to www.navpress.com to purchase.

To locate a Christian bookstore near you, call 1-800-991-7747.

NAVPRESS

BRINGING TRUTH TO LIFE

www.navpress.com